NIST Special Publication 800-57

Recommendation for Key Management – Part 2: Best Practices for Key Management Organization

NIST

**National Institute of
Standards and Technology**
Technology Administration
U.S. Department of Commerce

Elaine Barker, William Barker, William Burr, William Polk, and Miles Smid

C O M P U T E R   S E C U R I T Y

Abstract

Special Publication 800-57 provides cryptographic key management guidance. It consists of three parts. Part 1 provides general guidance and best practices for the management of cryptographic keying material. Part 2 provides guidance on policy and security planning requirements for U.S. government agencies. Finally, Part 3 provides guidance when using the cryptographic features of current systems.

KEY WORDS: accreditation; assurances; authentication; authorization; availability; backup; certification; compromise; confidentiality; cryptanalysis; cryptographic key; cryptographic module; digital signature; key management; key management policy; key recovery; private key; public key; public key infrastructure; security plan; trust anchor; validation.

Acknowledgements

The National Institute of Standards and Technology (NIST) gratefully acknowledges and appreciates contributions by Lydia Zieglar from the National Security Agency concerning the many security issues associated with this Recommendation. NIST also thanks the many contributions by the public and private sectors whose thoughtful and constructive comments improved the quality and usefulness of this publication.

Authority

This document has been developed by the National Institute of Standards and Technology (NIST) in furtherance of its statutory responsibilities under the Federal Information Security Management Act (FISMA) of 2002, Public Law 107-347.

NIST is responsible for developing standards and guidelines, including minimum requirements, for providing adequate information security for all agency operations and assets, but such standards and guidelines shall not apply to national security systems. This guideline is consistent with the requirements of the Office of Management and Budget (OMB) Circular A-130, Section 8b(3), Securing Agency Information Systems, as analyzed in A-130, Appendix IV: Analysis of Key Sections. Supplemental information is provided in A-130, Appendix III.

This guideline has been prepared for use by federal agencies. It may be used by nongovernmental organizations on a voluntary basis and is not subject to copyright. (Attribution would be appreciated by NIST.)

Nothing in this document should be taken to contradict standards and guidelines made mandatory and binding on federal agencies by the Secretary of Commerce under statutory authority. Nor should these guidelines be interpreted as altering or superseding the existing authorities of the Secretary of Commerce, Director of the OMB, or any other federal official.

Conformance testing for implementations of key management as specified in this Recommendation will be conducted within the framework of the Cryptographic Module Validation Program (CMVP), a joint effort of NIST and the Communications Security Establishment of the Government of Canada. Cryptographic implementations must adhere to the requirements in this Recommendation in order to be validated under the CMVP. The requirements of this Recommendation are indicated by the word "shall."

Overview

"Best Practices for Key Management Organization," Part 2 of the *Recommendation for Key Management* is intended primarily to address the needs of system owners and managers. It provides context, principles, and implementation guidelines to assist in implementation and management of institutional key management systems. It identifies applicable laws and directives concerning security planning and management, and suggests approaches to satisfying those laws and directives with a view to minimizing the impact of management overhead on organizational resources and efficiency. This guideline acknowledges that planning and documentation requirements associated with small scale or single system cryptographic applications will not need to be as elaborate as those required for large and diverse government agencies supported by a number of general support systems and major applications. However, any organization that employs cryptography to provide security services is required to have policy, practices and planning documentation at some level or number of levels.

Part 2 of the *Recommendation for Key Management* first identifies the structural and functional elements common to effective key management systems; second, identifies security planning requirements, general security policies and practices necessary to effective institutional key management; and finally, offers suggestions regarding how key management policies and procedures might be incorporated into security planning documentation that is already required by various Federal laws and directives.

The "Key Management Infrastructure," Section of Part 2 identifies the elements of a representative key management infrastructure and suggests functions of and relationships among the organizational elements. A more detailed representation of this general infrastructure is contained in Appendix A, "Notional Key Management Infrastructure." This "notional" infrastructure builds on the Public key infrastructure (PKI), Kerberos, and other US Government KMI components and mechanisms. It is noted that not all of the infrastructure elements will be implemented in the same way in all Federal institutions. Organizations with relatively simple and small-scale cryptographic requirements will be likely to bundle multiple functionality into single organizational elements in order to foster efficiency and economy. However, most of the functional elements identified in the notional infrastructure will need to be supported by some element of any key management organization.

Each U.S. Government organization that manages cryptographic systems that are intended to protect sensitive information **should** base the management of those systems on an organizational policy statement. The "Key Management Policy and Practices" subsection identifies U.S. Government laws, documents, and regulations relevant to the employment of cryptography and provides a sample structure and content for organizational Key Management Policies (KMP) and Key Management Practices Statements (KMPS). The KMPS specifies how key management procedures, and techniques are used to enforce the KMP.

The plans, practices, and/or procedures documents into which KMPs and KMPSs are inserted will vary from organization to organization. It is recommended that organizations create stand-

5

alone practices documents where required, but the key management practices information <u>may</u> be included in PKI Certification Practices Statements, the top-level information security policies, and/or security procedures documents. The practices information is more prescriptive and specific than the policy material, so the practices information will be subject to more frequent change than the policy information.

Key management controls required for Federal systems are identified in Special Publication 800-53, *Recommended Security Controls for Federal Information Systems*, National Institute of Standards and Technology, February 2005.

Key management information **should** be incorporated into security plans for general support systems and major applications that employ cryptography. These security plans are already required for general support systems and major applications by OMB Circular A-130. NIST Special Publication 800-18 Revision 1, Guide fo*r Developing Security Plans for Federal Information Systems*, provides suggested content for these system security plans. Key management-related additions to these plans are suggested in the "Information Technology System Security Plans" section of Part 2 of the *Recommendation for Key Management*, and templates for general support systems and major applications security plans are provided with key management enhancements as Appendix D.

Not all organizations and/or applications for which cryptography is desired are sufficiently large or complex to require system security plans for General Support Systems or Major Applications. The "Key Management Planning for Cryptographic Applications" section of Part 2 of the *Recommendation for Key Management* identifies Key Management information that needs to be documented for all Federal applications of cryptography.

Key generation, establishment, agreement, and transport mechanisms **shall** conform to FIPS 140-2. Data processing components of IT systems that support other key management functions may need to be evaluated under the *Common Criteria*. (See NIST Special Publication 800-23, *Guidelines to Federal Organizations on Security Assurance and Acquisition/Use of Tested/Evaluated Products*.) Where key management supports protection of sensitive Federal government information, the overall IT system including the set of systems that perform key management for a Federal government organization is subject to accreditation under SP 800-37, *Federal Guidelines for Security Certification and Accreditation of Information Systems*.

Table of Contents

RECOMMENDATION FOR KEY MANAGEMENT
Part 2: Best Practices for Key Management Organization

1. Introduction

"Best Practices for Key Management Organization," Part 2 of the *Recommendation for Key Management* is intended primarily to address the needs of system owners and managers. Parts 1 and 3 of the *Recommendation for Key Management* focus on technical key management mechanisms. Part 1, *General Guidance*, contains basic key management guidance intended to advise users, developers and system managers on the "best practices" associated with key management; and Part 3, *Application-Specific Key Management Guidance*, is intended to address the key management issues associated with currently available implementations. Technical mechanisms alone are not sufficient to ensure the protection of sensitive information. These mechanisms **shall** be used in combination with a set of procedures in order to implement a clearly understood and articulated protection policy. Part 2 provides a framework and general guidance to support establishing cryptographic key management policies, procedures, and the infrastructure within an organization as a basis for satisfying key management aspects of statutory and policy security planning requirements for Federal government organizations.

In acknowledgement of the heterogeneous nature of the cryptographic user community, the guideline presents a significant degree of flexibility with respect to the complexity of management infrastructures and the amount of documentation required to support key management. Planning and documentation requirements associated with small scale or single system cryptographic applications will obviously not be as elaborate as those required for large and diverse government agencies supported by a number of general support systems and major applications. However, any organization that employs cryptography to provide security services is likely to require policy, practices and planning documentation at some level or number of levels, and for a number of reasons.

- At the device or software application level, keying material needs to be provided, changed, and protected in a manner that enables cryptographic operation and preserves the integrity of cryptographic processes and their dependent services. FIPS 140-2 provides some guidance on implementing key entry functionality. A variety of government publications (e.g., NIST Special Publication 800-56, Recommendation on Key Establishment Schemes [SP800-56]) specify key establishment formats and processes in specific applications. This guideline specifies key management planning requirements for cryptographic product development and for applying or implementing cryptographic products in systems.

- At the systems level, planning is often required to enable the distribution of keying material in a manner that enables interoperability among cryptographic products employed in the system. Procedures for the acquisition, management, and protection of keying material are also required at the system level in order to preserve the integrity of cryptographic processes and their dependent services. This guideline specifies cryptographic and key management planning that needs to be incorporated into systems security plans for major applications and general support systems.

- At the organization level (e.g., government departmental and agency levels), planning is required to enable the acquisition or generation of keying material. Planning is also required to enable the distribution of keying material to systems operations activities in a manner that enables protected communications within the organization's systems, among the organization's systems, and with systems of other organizations as necessary to support the organization's mission requirements. Practices and procedures need to be specified at the organizational level to provide for the management and protection of keying material in order to preserve the integrity of cryptographic processes and their dependent services. This guideline specifies cryptographic and key management planning that needs to be documented and promulgated at the organizational level in order to implement and operate the key management infrastructure necessary to support the secure generation and/or acquisition, distribution, protection, and use of keying material that is consistent with product-level key specifications, system interoperability requirements, and the organization's mission.

- In order for key management practices and procedures to be effectively employed, support for these practices and procedures at the highest levels of the organization is a practical necessity. The executive level of the organization needs to establish policies that identify executive level key management roles and responsibilities for the organization. The key management policies need to support the establishment of, or access to, the services of a key management infrastructure and the employment and enforcement of key management practices and procedures.

1.1 Organization

Part 2 of the *Recommendation for Key Management* is organized as follows:

- Section 2 describes a generic key management infrastructure. The infrastructure description provides an organizational context for functions and responsibilities described in subsequent sections. The described infrastructure is an adaptation of the Public Key Infrastructure (PKI) and other widely employed key management infrastructures. Appendix A is a companion to Section 2 and details a notional Key Management Infrastructure (KMI) and establishes roles and relationships for the management of asymmetric and/or symmetric keying material in support of a broad range of cryptographic services. It is not anticipated that an organization will necessarily adopt all of the elements of the notional KMI as defined and described in this guideline. Unique organizations may significantly tailor the infrastructure elements, relationships, and terminology. Nevertheless, the basic functions and reporting responsibilities identified in Section 2 **should** be represented in organizational KMIs.

- Section 3 provides guidance for the development of organizational key management policy statements and key management practices statements. Key management policies and practices documentation may take the form of separate planning and implementation documents. Alternatively, the documentation may be included in an organization's existing information security policies and procedures.[1]

---

[1] Agency-wide security program plans are required by OMB guidance on implementing the *Government Information Security Reform Act*.

- Section 4 identifies key management information that **should** be incorporated into security plans for general support systems and major applications that employ cryptography.[2]

- Not all organizations and/or applications for which cryptography is desired are sufficiently large or complex to require system security plans for General Support Systems or Major Applications. Section 5 identifies Key Management information that needs to be documented for all Federal applications of cryptography.

1.2 Glossary of Terms and Acronyms

Definitions provided below are defined as used in the *Recommendation for Key Management*. The same terms may be defined differently in other documents.

1.2.1 Glossary

Access control	Restricts access to resources only to privileged entities.
Accountability	A property that ensures that the actions of an entity may be traced uniquely to that entity.
Approved	FIPS-Approved and/or NIST-recommended. An algorithm or technique that is either 1) specified in a FIPS or NIST Recommendation, or 2) adopted in a FIPS or NIST Recommendation and specified either in an appendix to the FIPS or NIST Recommendation, or in a document referenced by the FIPS or NIST Recommendation.
Archive	See Key management archive.
Association	A relationship for a particular purpose. For example, a key is associated with the application or process for which it will be used.
Asymmetric key algorithm	See Public key cryptographic algorithm.
Authentication	A process that establishes the origin of information, or determines an entity's identity. In a general information security context: Verifying the identity of a user, process, or device, often as a prerequisite to allowing access to resources in an information system [SP800-53].
Authentication code	A cryptographic checksum based on an Approved security function (also known as a Message Authentication Code).
Authority	The aggregate of people, procedures, documentation, hardware, and/or software necessary to authorize and enable security-relevant functions.

---

[2] These security plans are required for general support systems and major applications by OMB Circular A-130.

Authorization	Access privileges granted to an entity; conveys an "official" sanction to perform a security function or activity.
Availability	Timely, reliable access to information by authorized entities.
Backup	A copy of information to facilitate recovery, if necessary.
Central oversight authority	The Key Management Infrastructure (KMI) entity that provides overall KMI data synchronization and system security oversight for an organization or set of organizations.
Certificate	See public key certificate.
Certificate policy	A named set of rules that indicate the applicability of a certificate to a particular community and/or class of applications with common security requirements.
Certification authority (CA)	The entity in a Public Key Infrastructure (PKI) that is responsible for issuing certificates and exacting compliance to a PKI policy.
Certification practices statement	A statement of the practices that a certification authority employs in issuing certificates.
Ciphertext	Data in its encrypted form.
Compromise	The unauthorized disclosure, modification, substitution, or use of sensitive data (e.g., keying material and other security related information).
Confidentiality	The property that sensitive information is not disclosed to unauthorized entities. In a general information security context: preserving authorized restrictions on information access and disclosure, including means for preserving personal privacy and proprietary information [SP800-53].
Cross certification	Used by one CA to certify any CA other than a CA immediately adjacent (superior or subordinate) to it in a CA hierarchy.
Cryptanalysis	1. Operations performed in defeating cryptographic protection without an initial knowledge of the key employed in providing the protection. 2. The study of mathematical techniques for attempting to defeat cryptographic techniques and information system security. This includes the process of looking for errors or weaknesses in the implementation of an algorithm or of the algorithm itself.
Cryptographic key (key)	A parameter used in conjunction with a cryptographic algorithm that determines its operation in such a way that an entity with knowledge of the key can reproduce or reverse the operation, while an entity without knowledge of the key cannot. Examples include:

- the transformation of plaintext data into ciphertext data,

- the transformation of ciphertext data into plaintext data,

- the computation of a digital signature from data,

- the verification of a digital signature,

- the computation of an authentication code from data,

- the computation of a shared secret that is used to derive keying material.

Cryptographic key component (key component)	One of at least two parameters that have the same format as a cryptographic key; parameters are combined in an Approved security function to form a plaintext cryptographic key before use.
Cryptographic module	The set of hardware, software, and/or firmware that implements Approved security functions (including cryptographic algorithms and key generation) and is contained within the cryptographic boundary.
Cryptoperiod	The time span during which a specific key is authorized for use or in which the keys for a given system or application may remain in effect.
Data key, Data encrypting key	A cryptographic key that is used to cryptographically protect data (e.g., encrypt, decrypt, authenticate).
Data integrity	A property whereby data has not been altered in an unauthorized manner since it was created, transmitted, or stored.
Data origin authentication	Corroborating that the source of the data is as claimed.
Decryption	The process of changing ciphertext into plaintext using a cryptographic algorithm and key.
Destruction	The process of overwriting, erasing, or physically destroying a key so that it cannot be recovered.
Digital signature	The result of a cryptographic transformation of data that, when properly implemented, provides the services of: 1. origin authentication 2. data integrity, and 3. signer non-repudiation.
Distribution	See key distribution.
Dual control	A process that uses two or more separate entities (usually persons) operating in concert to protect sensitive functions or information. No single entity is able to access or use the materials, e.g., cryptographic keys.

Encrypted key	A cryptographic key that has been encrypted using an Approved security function with a key encrypting key in order to disguise the value of the underlying plaintext key.
Encryption	The process of changing plaintext into ciphertext using a cryptographic algorithm and key.
Initialization vector (IV)	A vector used in defining the starting point of an encryption process within a cryptographic algorithm.
Integrity	In the general information security context: guarding against improper modification and includes ensuring information non-repudiation and authenticity [SP800-53]. In a cryptographic context: the property that sensitive data has not been modified or deleted in an unauthorized and undetected manner.
Integrity detection	The detection of modifications to data.
Integrity restoration	The restoration of the data to its original contents when modifications have been detected.
Key de-registration	A stage in the lifecycle of keying material; the removal of records of keying material that was registered by a registration authority.
Key distribution	The transport of a key and other keying material from an entity that either owns the key or generates the key to another entity that is intended to use the key.
Key encrypting key	A cryptographic key that is used for the encryption or decryption of other keys.
Key establishment	A stage in the lifecycle of keying material; the process by which cryptographic keys are securely distributed among cryptographic modules using manual transport methods (e.g., key loaders), automated methods (e.g., key transport and/or key agreement protocols), or a combination of automated and manual methods (consists of key transport plus key agreement).
Keying material installation	A stage in the lifecycle of keying material; the installation of keying material for operational use.
Key management	The activities involving the handling of cryptographic keys and other related security parameters (e.g., IVs and passwords) during the entire life cycle of the keys, including their generation, storage, establishment, entry and output, and destruction.
Key management infrastructure	The framework and services that provide for the generation, production, distribution, control, accounting, and destruction of all cryptographic material, including symmetric keys, as well as public keys and public key certificates. It includes all elements (hardware, software, other equipment, and documentation); facilities; personnel;

procedures; standards; and information products that form the system that distributes, manages, and supports the delivery of cryptographic products and services to end users.

Key management plan	The Key Management Plan is the document that describes for a cryptographic device or application the management of all key management products and services distributed by the Key Management Infrastructure and employed by that cryptographic device or application. The Key Management Plan documents how current and/or planned key management products and services will be supplied by the Key Management Infrastructure and used by the cryptographic application to ensure that lifecycle key management support is available.
Key management policy	The Key Management Policy is a high-level statement of organizational key management policies that identifies high-level structure, responsibilities, governing standards and guidelines, organizational dependencies and other relationships, and security policies.
Key management product	A key management product is a cryptographic key (symmetric or asymmetric) or certificate used for encryption, decryption, digital signature, or signature verification; and other items, such as certificate revocation lists and compromised key lists, obtained by trusted means from the same source, which validate the authenticity of keys or certificates. Software that performs either a security or cryptographic function (e.g., keying material accounting and control, random number generation, cryptographic module verification) is also considered to be a cryptographic product.
Key management practices statement	The Key Management Practices Statement is a document or set of documentation that describes in detail the organizational structure, responsible roles, and organization rules for the functions identified in the Key Management Policy.
Key management service	A key management service is a function performed for or by an existing key management module. Examples are key ordering, distribution, re-key, update of keying material attributes, and certificate revocation. Other cryptographic services include key recovery and the distribution, accounting, tracking, and control of software that performs either keying material security or cryptographic functions.
Key pair	A public key and its corresponding private key; a key pair is used with a public key algorithm.
Key processing facility	The Key Processing Facility is a KMI component that performs one or more of the following functions:

- Acquisition or generation of public key certificates,

16

- Initial generation and distribution of keying material,

- Maintenance of a database that maps user entities to an organization's certificate/key structure,

- Maintenance and distribution of nodal key compromise lists and/or certificate revocation lists, and

- Generation of audit requests and the processing audit responses as necessary for the prevention of undetected compromises.

Key recovery	A stage in the lifecycle of keying material; mechanisms and processes that allow authorized entities to retrieve keying material from key backup or archive.
Key registration	A stage in the lifecycle of keying material; the process of officially recording the keying material by a registration authority.
Key revocation	A stage in the lifecycle of keying material; a process whereby a notice is made available to affected entities that keying material **should** be removed from operational use prior to the end of the established cryptoperiod of that keying material.
Key specification	A key specification documents the data format, encryption algorithms, hashing algorithms, signature algorithms, physical media, and data constraints for keys required by a cryptographic device and/or application.
Key transport	Secure transport of cryptographic keys from one cryptographic module to another module. When used in conjunction with a public key (asymmetric) algorithm, keying material is encrypted using a public key and subsequently decrypted using a private key. When used in conjunction with a symmetric algorithm, key transport is known as key wrapping.
Key update	A stage in the lifecycle of keying material; alternate storage for operational keying material during its cryptoperiod.
Key wrapping	Encrypting a symmetric key using another symmetric key (the key encrypting key). A key used for key wrapping is known as a key encrypting key.
Keying material	The data (e.g., keys and IVs) necessary to establish and maintain cryptographic keying relationships.
Label	Information that either identifies an associated parameter or provides information regarding the parameter's proper protection and use.
Least privilege	A security principle that restricts the access privileges of authorized personnel (e.g., program execution privileges, file modification privileges) to the minimum necessary to perform their jobs.

Non-repudiation	A service that is used to provide assurance of the integrity and origin of data in such a way that the integrity and origin can be verified by a third party as having originated from a specific entity in possession of the private key of the claimed signatory. In a general information security context, assurance that the sender of information is provided with proof of delivery and the recipient is provided with proof of the sender's identity, so neither can later deny having processed the information [SP800-53].
Password	A string of characters (letters, numbers and other symbols) that are used to authenticate an identity or to verify access authorization.
Plaintext	Intelligible data that has meaning and can be understood without the application of decryption.
Private key	A cryptographic key, used with a public key cryptographic algorithm that is uniquely associated with an entity and is not made public. In an asymmetric (public) cryptosystem, the private key is associated with a public key. The private key is known only by the owner of the key pair and is used to:

1. Compute the corresponding public key,

2. Compute a digital signature that may be verified by the corresponding public key,

3. Decrypt data that was encrypted by the corresponding public key, or

4. Compute a piece of common shared data, together with other information.

Public key	A cryptographic key used with a public key cryptographic algorithm that is uniquely associated with an entity and that may be made public. In an asymmetric (public) cryptosystem, the public key is associated with a private key. The public key may be known by anyone and is used to:

1. Verify a digital signature that is signed by the corresponding private key,

2. Encrypt data that can be decrypted by the corresponding private key, or

3. Compute a piece of shared data.

Public key certificate	A set of data that uniquely identifies an entity, contains the entity's public key and possibly other information, and is digitally signed by a trusted party, thereby binding the public key to the entity. Additional information in the certificate could specify how the key is used and its cryptoperiod.

Public key (asymmetric) cryptographic algorithm	A cryptographic algorithm that uses two related keys, a public key and a private key. The two keys have the property that determining the private key from the public key is computationally infeasible.
Public Key Infrastructure (PKI)	A framework that is established to issue, maintain and revoke public key certificates.
Random Number Generator (RNG)	Produces a sequence of zero and one bits that is random in the sense, that there is no way to describe its output that is more efficient than simply listing the entire string of output. There are two basic classes: deterministic and non-deterministic. A deterministic RNG (also known as a pseudorandom number generator) consists of an algorithm that produces a sequence of bits from an initial value called a seed. A non-deterministic RNG produces output that is dependent on some unpredictable physical source that is outside human control, such as thermal noise or radioactive decay.
Registration Authority (RA)	An entity that is responsible for the identification and authentication of certificate subjects on behalf of an authority, but that does not sign or issue certificates (e.g., an RA is delegated certain tasks on behalf of a CA).
Relying party	An entity that relies on received information for authentication purposes.
Secret key	A cryptographic key that is used with a secret key (also known as a symmetric key) cryptographic algorithm that is uniquely associated with one or more entities and **shall not** be made public. The use of the term "secret" in this context does not imply a classification level, but rather implies the need to protect the key from disclosure.
Security policy	Defines the threats that a system **shall** address and provides high-level mechanisms for addressing those threats.
Security services	Mechanisms used to provide confidentiality, data integrity, authentication or non-repudiation of information.
Separation of duties	A security principle that divides critical functions among different staff members in an attempt to ensure that no one individual has enough information or access privilege to perpetrate damaging fraud.
Service agents	Entities that support organizations' KMIs as single points of access for other KMI nodes.
Subject Certification Authority	In the context of a particular CA certificate, the CA whose public key is certified in the certificate.
Symmetric key	A single cryptographic key that is shared by both originator and recipient (see symmetric key algorithm)

recipient (see symmetric key algorithm).

Symmetric key algorithm	A cryptographic algorithm that employs one shared key, a secret key.
Threat	Any circumstance or event with the potential to adversely impact agency operations (including mission function, image, or reputation), agency assets or individuals through an information system via unauthorized access, destruction, disclosure, modification of data, and/or denial of service [SP800-53].
Unauthorized disclosure	An event involving the exposure of information to entities not authorized access to the information.
X.509 certificate	Public key certificates that contain three nested elements: 1) the tamper-evident envelope (digitally signed by the source), 2) the basic certificate content (e.g., identifying information and public key), and 3) extensions that contain optional certificate information.
Zeroization	A method of erasing electronically stored data, cryptographic keys, and critical stored parameters by altering or deleting the contents of the data storage to prevent recovery of the data.

1.2.2   Acronyms

The following abbreviations and acronyms are used in this standard:

CA	Certification Authority
CIO	Chief Information Officer
CKL	Compromised Key List
CN	Client Node
COA	Central Oversight Authority
CPS	Certification Practices Statement
CP	Certificate Policy
CRL	Certificate Revocation List
CSN	Central Service Node
FIPS	Federal Information Processing Standard.
KMI	Key Management Infrastructure
KMP	Key Management Policy
KMPS	Key Management Practices Statement

KPF	Key Processing Facility
NIST	National Institute of Standards and Technology
OMB	Office of Management and Budget
PKI	Public Key Infrastructure
PRNG	Pseudorandom Number Generator
RA	Registration Authority
RNG	Random Number Generator
SA	Service Agent

2   Key Management Infrastructure

The complexity of and allocation of roles within a key management infrastructure will depend on 1) the cryptographic algorithms employed, 2) the operational and communications relationships among the organizational elements being served, 3) the purposes for which cryptography is employed, and 4) the number and complexity of cryptographic relationships required by an organization.   This section identifies common key management infrastructure elements and suggests functions of and relationships among the organizational elements. In Appendix A, these elements and functions are organized into a "notional" key management infrastructure (KMI) that builds on the Public key infrastructure (PKI), Kerberos, and US Government KMI components and mechanisms. The notional KMI is employed to illustrate distribution and management of symmetric and asymmetric keys in a hierarchical organization.

The structure, complexity, and scale of actual KMIs may vary considerably according to the needs of individual organizations. However, the elements and functions identified here need to be present in most organizations that require cryptographic protection. This subsection describes the common KMI organizational elements, functions, and requirements.

A KMI is designed to incorporate a set of functional elements, or nodes, that collectively provide unified and seamless protection policy enforcement and key management services. Four distinct functional nodes are identified for the generation, distribution, and management of cryptographic keys: a central oversight authority, key processing facility(ies), service agents, and client nodes. It should be noted that organizations may choose to combine the functionality of more than one node into a single component. Figure 1 illustrates functional KMI relationships.

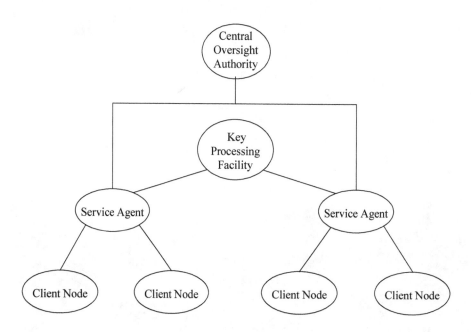

Figure 1: KMI Components

22

2.1 Central Oversight Authority

The KMI's central oversight authority is the entity that provides overall KMI data synchronization and system security oversight for an organization or set of organizations. The central oversight authority 1) coordinates protection policy and practices (procedures) documentation, 2) may function as a holder of data provided by service agents, and 3) serves as the source for common and system level information required by service agents (e.g., keying material and registration information, directory data, system policy specifications, and system-wide key compromise and certificate revocation information). As required by survivability or continuity of operations policies, central oversight facilities may be replicated at an appropriate remote site to function as a system back up.

2.2 Key Processing Facility(ies)

Key processing services typically include one or more of the following:

- Acquisition or generation of public key certificates (where applicable),

- Initial generation and distribution of keying material,

- Maintenance of a database that maps user entities to an organization's certificate/key structure,

- Maintenance and distribution of compromise key lists (CKLs) and/or certificate revocation lists (CRLs), and

- Generation of audit requests and the processing of audit responses as necessary for the prevention of undetected compromises.

An organization may use more than one key processing facility to provide these services (e.g., for purposes of inter-organizational interoperation). Key processing facilities can be added to meet new requirements or deleted when no longer needed and may support both public key and symmetric key establishment techniques.

Where public key cryptography is employed, the organization operating the key processing facility will generally perform most PKI registration authority, repository, and archive functions. The organization also performs at least some PKI certification authority functions. Actual X.509 public key certificates may be obtained from a government source (certification authorities generating identification, attribute, or encryption certificates) or a commercial external certification authority (usually a commercial infrastructure/CA that supplies/sells X.509 certificates). Commercial external certification authority certificates **should** be cross-certified by a government root CA.

A key processing facility may be distributed such that intermediary redistribution facilities maintain stores of keying material that exist in physical form (e.g., magnetic media, smart cards) and may also serve as a source for non-cryptographic products and services (e.g., software downloads for KMI-reliant users, usage documents, or policy authority).

All keys and non-cryptographic products that are electronically distributed to end users **shall** be encrypted for the end user or for intermediary redistribution services before transmission. Some key processing facilities may generate and produce human-readable key information and other key-related information that require physical distribution. Keys that are manually distributed

shall either be encrypted or receive physical protection and be subject to controlled distribution (e.g., registered mail) between the key processing facility and the user. Part 1, Section 2.3.1 provides general guidance for key distribution. Newly deployed key processing facilities **should** be designed to support legacy and existing system requirements and **should** be designed to support future network services as they become available.

2.3   Service Agents

Service agents support organizations' KMIs as single points of access for other KMI nodes. All transactions initiated by client nodes are either processed by a service agent or forwarded to other nodes for processing. Service agents direct service requests from client nodes to key processing facilities, and when services are required from multiple processing facilities, coordinate services among the processing facilities to which they are connected. Service agents are employed by users to order keying material and services, retrieve keying material and services, and manage cryptographic material and public key certificates. A service agent may provide cryptographic material and/or certificates by utilizing specific key processing facilities for key and/or certificate generation. A service agent that supports a major organizational unit or geographic region may either access a central or inter-organizational key processing facility or employ local, dedicated processing facilities as required to support survivability, performance, or availability, requirements (e.g., a commercial external Certificate Authority).

Service agents may provide registration, directory, and support for data recovery services (i.e. key recovery), as well as provide access to relevant documentation, such as policy statements and infrastructure devices. Service agents may also process requests for keying material (e.g., user identification credentials), and assign and manage KMI user roles and privileges. A service agent may also provide interactive help desk services as required.

2.4   Client Nodes

Client nodes are interfaces for managers, devices, and applications to access KMI functions, including the requesting of certificates and other keying material. They may include cryptographic modules, software, and procedures necessary to provide user access to the KMI. Client nodes interact with service agents to obtain cryptographic key services. Client nodes provide interfaces to end user entities (e.g., encryption devices) for the distribution of keying material, for the generation of requests for keying material, for the receipt and forwarding (as appropriate) of compromised key lists (CKLs) and/or certificate revocation lists (CRLs), for the receipt of audit requests, and for the delivery of audit responses. Client nodes typically initiate requests for keying material in order to synchronize new or existing user entities with the current key structure, and receive encrypted keying material for distribution to end-user cryptographic devices (in which the content - the unencrypted keying material – is not usually accessible to human users or user-node interface processes). A client node can be a FIPS 140-2 compliant workstation executing KMI security software or a FIPS 140-2 compliant special purpose device. Actual interactions between a client node and a service agent depend on whether the client node is a device, a manager, or a functional security application. Examples of different types of client nodes and their relationships to service agents are provided in Appendix A.

3 Key Management Policy and Practices

A key management policy is a set of rules that are established to describe the goals, responsibilities, and overall requirements for the management of cryptographic keying material used to protect private or critical facilities, processes, or information. Key Management Policies (KMP) are implemented through a combination of security mechanisms and procedures. An organization uses security mechanisms (e.g., safes, alarms, random number generators, encryption algorithms, signature and authentication algorithms) as tools to implement a policy. However, key management mechanisms will produce the desired results only if they are properly configured and maintained. Key Management Practices Statements (KMPS) document the procedures that system administrators and users follow when establishing and maintaining key management mechanisms and when using cryptographic systems. The procedures documented in the KMPS describe are how the security requirements described in the KMP are met and are directly linked to the key management mechanisms employed by an organization. [PKI 01]

U. S. Government agencies that use cryptography are responsible for defining the KMP that governs the lifecycle for the cryptographic keys as specified in Part 1, Section 2.3 of the *Recommendation for Key Management*. A KMPS is then developed, based on the KMP and the actual applications supported.

Policy and practices documentation requirements associated with small scale or single system cryptographic applications will obviously not be as elaborate as those required for large and diverse government agencies that are supported by a number of general support systems and major applications. However, any organization that employs cryptography to provide security services is likely to require some level of policy, practices and planning documentation.

3.1 Key Management Policy (KMP)

Each U.S. Government organization that manages cryptographic systems that are intended to protect sensitive information **should** base the management of those systems on an organizational policy statement. The KMP[3] is a high-level document that describes authorization and protection objectives and constraints that apply to the generation, distribution, accounting, storage, use, and destruction of cryptographic keying material.

3.1.2 Policy Content

The Key Management Policy (KMP) is a high-level statement of organizational key management policies that includes authorization and protection objectives, and constraints that apply to the generation, distribution, accounting, storage, use, and destruction of cryptographic keying material. The policy document or documents that comprise the KMP will include high-level key management structure and responsibilities, governing standards and guidelines, organizational dependencies and other relationships, and security objectives. [Note that in a purely PKI environment, the KMP is usually a stand-alone document known as a Certificate Policy (CP).]

---

[3] In a purely PKI environment, the KMP may be a Certificate Policy (CP) in conformance to RFC 3647, the Internet X.509 Public Key Infrastructure Certificate Policy and Certification Practices Framework [RFC3647].

The scope of a KMP may be limited to the operation of a single PKI Certificate Authority (CA) and its supporting components[4], or to a symmetric point-to-point or single key center environment.[5] Alternatively, the scope of a KMP may be the operations of a hierarchical PKI, bridged PKI, or multiple center symmetric key environment.

The KMP is used for a number of different purposes. The KMP is used to guide the development of KMPSs for each PKI CA or symmetric key management group that operates under its provisions. CAs from other organizations' PKIs may review the KMP before cross-certification, and managers of symmetric key KMIs may review the KMP before joining new or existing multiple center groups. Auditors and accreditors will use the KMP as the basis for their reviews of PKI CA and/or symmetric key KMI operations. Application owners that are considering a PKI certificate source **should** review a KMP/CP to determine whether its certificates are appropriate for their applications.

3.1.2.1 General Policy Content Requirements

Although detailed formats are specified for some environments (e.g., See Appendix B for a PKI CP format), the policy documents into which key management information is inserted may vary from organization to organization. In general, the information **should** appear in a top-level organizational information systems policies and practices document. The policy need not always be elaborate. A degree of flexibility may be desirable with respect to actual organizational assignments and operations procedures in order to accommodate organizational and information infrastructure changes over time. However, the KMP needs to establish a policy foundation for the full set of key management functions.

3.1.2.1.1 Security Objectives

A KMP **should** state the security objectives that are applicable to and expected to be supported by the KMI. The security objectives **should** include the identification of:

(a) The nature of the information to be protected (e.g., financial transactions, confidential information, critical process data);

(b) The classes of threats against which protection is required (e.g., the unauthorized modification of data, replay of communications, fraudulent repudiation of transactions, disclosure of information to unauthorized parties);

(c) The Federal Information Processing Standard 199 (FIPS 199) impact level which is determined by the consequences of a compromise of the protected information and/or processes (including sensitivity and perishability of the information);

(d) The cryptographic protection mechanisms to be employed (e.g., message authentication, digital signature, encryption);

(e) Protection requirements for cryptographic processes and keying material (e.g., tamper-resistant processes, confidentiality of keying material); and

---

[4] This is generally the case when a single CA serves an enterprise or a CA participates in a mesh. [PKI 01]

[5] Note that multiple CAs and/or single symmetric point-to-point or center groups may operate under a single KMP.

(f) Applicable statutes, and executive directives and guidance to which the KMI and its supporting documentation **shall** conform.

The statement of security objectives will provide a basis and justification for other provisions of the KMP.

3.1.2.1.2 Organizational Responsibilities

The KMP **should** identify key KMI management responsibilities and roles, including organizational contact information. The following classes of organizational responsibilities **should** be identified:

(a) <u>Identification of the Keying Material Manager</u> – Since the security of all material that is cryptographically protected depends on the security of the keying material employed, the ultimate responsibility for key management **should** reside at the executive level. The keying material manager **should** report directly to the organization's Chief Information Officer (CIO).[6] The keying material manager is a key employee who **should** have been determined to have the capabilities and trustworthiness that are commensurate with the responsibility for maintaining the authority and integrity of all formal, electronic transactions and the confidentiality of all information that is sufficiently sensitive to warrant cryptographic protection. Where public key cryptography is employed, either the keying material manager or his/her immediate superior **should** be designated as the organization's certification authority.

(b) <u>Identification of Infrastructure Entities and Roles</u> - The key management policy document **should** identify organizational responsibilities for key KMI roles. The following roles (where applicable to the type and complexity of the infrastructure being established[7]) **should** be assigned:

    (1) Central Oversight Authority (may be the Keying Material Manager)

    (2) Certification Authorities (CAs)

    (3) Registration Authorities (RAs)

    (4) Overseers of operations (e.g., Key Processing Facility(ies), Service Agents)

(c) <u>Basis for and Identification of Essential Key Management Roles</u> – The KMP **should** also identify responsible organization(s), organization (not individual) contact information, and any relevant statutory or administrative requirements for the following functions:

    (1) Key generation or acquisition;

    (2) Agreements with partner organizations regarding the cross certification of keying material and/or key establishment, as appropriate;

    (3) Key establishment and revocation tree design and management,

---

[6] When an organization does not have a CIO position, FISMA requires the associated responsibilities to be handled by a comparable agency official.

[7] E.g., PKI, KMI for multiple center symmetric key distribution.

(4) Establishment of cryptoperiods;

(5) Distribution of and accounting for keying material;

(6) Protection of secret and private keys and related materials;

(7) Emergency and routine revocation of keying material;

(8) Auditing of keying material and related records;

(9) Destruction of revoked or expired keys;

(10) Key recovery;

(11) Compromise recovery;

(12) Contingency planning,

(13) Disciplinary consequences for the willful or negligent mishandling of keying material; and

(14) Generation, approval, and maintenance of key management practices statements.

3.1.2.1.3 Sample KMP Format

The sample format provided in this subsection is designed to be compatible with the Standard Format for PKI Certificate Policies (Appendix B). The sample format differs somewhat from that for PKI Certificate Policies (CPs) because some key management characteristics of and requirements for KMIs that accommodate symmetric keys differ from those for purely PKI-based KMIs. The sample KMP format includes the general information called for in Subsections 3.1.2.1.1 and 3.1.2.1.2 above, plus some additional material that may be required in some administrative environments. As stated above, variations among organizational structures and needs will necessarily result in variations in the form and content of policy documentation. The sample KMP format is provided as a general guide rather than as a mandatory template.

(a) *Introduction* -

The *Introduction* identifies and introduces the provisions of the policy document and indicates the security objectives and the types of entities and applications for which the KMP is targeted. This section has the following subsections: 1) Overview, 2) Identification, 3) Community and Applicability, and 4) Contact Details.

Overview - This subsection introduces the KMP.

Objectives – This subsection states the security objectives applicable to and expected to be supported by the KMI. The *Objectives* subsection **should** include the elements information called for in Section 3.1.2.1.1 above (Security Objectives). [Note that in the case of a CP for a purely PKI environment, the *Overview* is followed by an *Identification* subsection that provides any applicable names or other identifiers, including ASN.1 object identifiers, for the set of policy provisions.]

Community and Applicability - This subsection identifies the types of entities that distribute keys or certificates. In the general case of the KMI, this will include the responsible entities identified in the "Identification of Infrastructure Entities and Roles" element of Section 3.1.2.1.2 above (Organizational Responsibilities). [Note that in the case of a KMI that includes a PKI CA, this subsection **should** identify the types of entities that issue certificates or that are certified as subject CAs, the types of entities that perform RA functions, and the types of entities that are certified as subject end entities or subscribers.] This subsection may also contains:

- A list of applications for which the issued certificates and/or identified key types are suitable. (Examples of application in this case are: electronic mail, retail transactions, contracts, travel order, etc.)

- A list of applications to which the use of the issued certificates and/or identified key types is restricted. (This list implicitly prohibits all other uses for the certificates.)

- A list of applications for which the use of the issued certificates and/or identified key types is prohibited.

Contact Details - This subsection includes the organization, telephone number, and mailing and/or network address of the Keying Material Manager. This is the authority responsible for the registration, maintenance, and interpretation of the KMP (see Section 3.1.2.1.1).

(b) *General Provisions* –

The *General Provisions* section of the KMP identifies any applicable policies regarding a range of legal and general practices topics. This section may contain subsections covering 1) obligations, 2) liability, 3) financial responsibility, 4) interpretation and enforcement, 5) fees, 6) publication and repositories, 7) compliance audit, 8) confidentiality, and 9) intellectual property rights. Each subcomponent may need to separately state the provisions applying to each KMI entity type (e.g., central oversight authority, key processing facility, service agent, client node, PKI CA, PKI repository, PKI RA, PKI subscriber, and/or PKI relying party[8]).

Obligations - This subsection contains, for each entity type, any applicable policies regarding the entity's obligations to other entities. Such provisions may include: 1) Keying Material Manager and/or Central Oversight Authority obligations, 2) Key Processing Facility obligations, 3) Service Agent obligations, 4) CA and/or RA obligations (PKI), 4) User obligations (including Client Nodes and PKI subscribers and relying parties), and 5) Keying Material Repository obligations.

Liability - This subsection contains, for each entity type, any applicable policies regarding the apportionment of liability (e.g., warranties and limitations on warranties, kinds of damages covered and disclaimers, loss limitations per certificate or per transaction, and other exclusions like acts of God).

---

[8] Specific provisions regarding subscribers and relying parties are only applicable in the Liability and Obligations subcomponents.

Financial Responsibility - This subsection contains, for key and/or certificate providers (e.g., key processing facilities, key distribution or translation centers, PKI CAs, key or certificate repositories, PKI RAs), any applicable policies regarding financial responsibilities, such as 1) the indemnification of KMI provider entity relying parties, 2) fiduciary relationships (or lack thereof) among the various entities; and 3) administrative processes (e.g., accounting, audit).

Interpretation and Enforcement - This subsection contains any applicable policies regarding the interpretation and enforcement of the KMP or KMPS, addressing such topics as 1) governing law; 2) the severability of provisions, survival, merger, and notice; and 3) dispute resolution procedures.

Fees - This subsection contains any applicable policies regarding interagency reimbursement or fees charged by key variable and/or certificate providers (e.g., reimbursement for key center management, certificate issuance or renewal fees, a certificate access fee, revocation or status information access fee, reimbursement for information desk services, fees for other services such as policy information, refund policy).

Publication and Repositories - This subsection contains any applicable policies regarding 1) a key and/or certificate source's obligations to publish information regarding its practices, its products (e.g., keys, certificates), and the current status of such products; 2) the frequency of publication; 3) access control on published information (e.g., policies, practice statements, key variables, certificates, key variable and/or certificate status, CRLs, CKLs); and 4) requirements pertaining to the use of repositories operated by private sector CAs or by other independent parties.

Compliance Audit - This subsection addresses any high-level policies regarding 1) the frequency of compliance audit for KMI entities, 2) the identity/qualifications of the auditor, 3) the auditor's relationship to the entity being audited, 4) topics covered under the compliance audit[9], 5) actions taken as a result of a deficiency found during compliance audit, 6) the dissemination of compliance audit results.

Confidentiality Policy - This subsection states policies regarding 1) the types of information that **shall** be kept confidential by KMI entities, 2) the types of information that are not considered confidential, 3) the dissemination of reasons for revocation and suspension of certificates, 4) the release of information to law enforcement officials, 5) information that can be revealed as part of civil discovery, 6) the disclosure of keys or certificates by KMI entities at subscriber/user request; and 7) any other circumstances under which confidential information may be disclosed.

Intellectual Property Rights - This subsection addresses policies concerning the ownership rights of certificates, practice/policy specifications, names, and keys.

---

[9] May be by reference to audit guidelines documents.

(c) *Identification and Authentication* –

The *Identification and Authentication* section describes circumstances and identifies any applicable regulatory authority and guidelines regarding the authentication of a certificate applicant or key variable requestor prior to the issuing of key(s) or certificate(s) by a keying material source. This section also includes policies regarding the authentication of parties requesting re-key or revocation. Where applicable, this section also addresses PKI naming practices, including name ownership recognition and name dispute resolution. This section of the KMP has the following subsections:

- Initial Registration,
- Routine Re-key,
- Re-key After Revocation, and
- Revocation Request.

(d) *Operational Requirements* –

The *Operational Requirements* section specifies policies regarding the imposition of requirements on KMI entities with respect to various operational activities. This section may address the following topics:

- Request for shared key variable relationship/Certificate application,
- Initial issuance of key encrypting keys and/or Certificate issuance,
- Acceptance of key variables and Certificates,
- Key and/or Certificate suspension and revocation,
- Security audit requirements,
- Records archiving,
- Key changeover (including re-keying, updating, re-derivation),
- Compromise and disaster recovery, and
- Key Center and/or CA Termination.

Within each topic, separate consideration may need to be given to each KMI entity class.

(e) *Minimum Baseline Security Controls* –

This section states policies regarding management, operational, and technical security controls (i.e., physical, procedural, and personnel controls) used by KMI components to securely perform 1) key generation, 2) subject authentication, 3) key establishment/transfer and/or certificate issuance, 4) key and/or certificate revocation, 5) audit, and 6) archiving.

Based on the FIPS 199 impact level, the appropriate minimum baseline of security controls contained in NIST Special Publication 800-53, *Recommended Security Controls for Federal Information Systems*, **shall** be implemented and described in this section of the KMP.

(f) *Cryptographic Key, Message Interchange, and/or Certificate Formats* –

This section is used to state policies specifying conformance to specific standards and/or guidelines regarding 1) key management architectures and/or protocols, 2) key management message formats, 3) certificate formats and/or 4) CRL/CKL formats.

(g) *Specification and Administration* –

The "Specification Administration" section of the policy document specifies:

- What organization(s) has/have change control responsibility for the KMP,

- Publication and notification procedures for new versions, and

- KMPS approval procedures.

3.1.3   Policy Enforcement

In order to be effective, key management policies **shall** be enforced, and policy implementation **should** be evaluated on a regular basis. Appendix C provides an evaluator's checklist for the documentation and practices that implement key management policies.

Of course, evaluation requirements will vary with the size and complexity of an organization's protected communications infrastructure. Each organization will need to determine its requirements based on the sensitivity of information being exchanged, the communications volume associated with sensitive or critical information and processes, personnel resources, the size and complexity of the organization or organizations supported, the variety and numbers of cryptographic devices and applications, the types of cryptographic devices and applications, and the scale and complexity of protected communications facilities.

3.2   Key Management Practices Statement (KMPS)

The Key Management Practices Statement (KMPS) establishes a trust root for the KMI and specifies how key management procedures, and techniques are used to enforce the KMP. For example, a KMP might state that secret and private keys **shall** be protected from unauthorized disclosure. The corresponding KMPS might then state that secret and private keys **shall** be either encrypted or physically protected, and that it is the responsibility of the network systems administrator to ensure that the keys are properly safeguarded. (The KMPS would also identify and provide contact information for the network systems administrator.) Note that the practices information contained in a KMPS is more prescriptive and specific than policy material contained in a KMP, so it will be subject to more frequent change. Several KMPSs may implement a KMP for a single organization, one for each organizational key management domain (e.g., one for each of several CAs).

3.2.1   Alternative KMPS Formats

As in the case of the policy documentation, the plans, practices, and/or procedures documents into which KMPSs are inserted will vary from organization to organization. In general, the nature and complexity of the KMPS will vary with an organization's existing documentation requirements and the size and complexity of an organization's protected communications infrastructure. Each organization will need to determine its requirements based on the sensitivity of information being exchanged, the communications volume associated with sensitive or critical information and processes, personnel resources, the size and complexity of the organization or organizations supported, the variety and numbers of cryptographic devices and applications, types of cryptographic devices and applications, and the scale and complexity of protected communications facilities.

Each KMPS applies to a single KMI or a single domain of that KMI. The KMPS may be considered the overall operations manual for the KMI. Specific portions of the KMPS may be extracted to form a KMI Operations Guide, a CA Operations Guide, a Service Agent Manual, a Key Distribution Center Manual, a Key Translation Center Manual, an RA Manual, a PKI Users Guide, or other role-specific documentation. Auditors and accreditors may use the KMPS to supplement the KMP during reviews of KMI operations.

3.2.1.1   Stand-Alone KMPS

While it is recommended that organizations create stand-alone practices documents, the key management practices information may be included in pre-existing top-level organizational information security policies and/or security procedures documents. A stand-alone KMPS may follow the general RFC 3647 format described for the KMP in Section 3.1.2.1.3 above (Sample KMP Format), or it may follow a proprietary format. If the general outline of the sample KMP format is followed, the authors of the KMP will need to keep in mind the basic differences in character between a KMP and a KMPS. While the KMP is a high-level document that describes a security policy for issuing certificates and maintaining certificate status information, the KMPS is a highly detailed document that describes how a KMI implements a specific KMP. The KMPS identifies the KMP that it implements and specifies the mechanisms and procedures that are used to support the security policy. Where the KMP specifies organizational roles and states requirements for mechanisms and procedures, the KMPS identifies the specific individuals assigned to each role and describes the mechanisms and procedures in detail. [Note that descriptive material can sometimes be included by reference to other procedures, guidelines, and/or standards documents.] The KMPS **should** include sufficient operational detail to demonstrate that the KMP can be satisfied by this combination of mechanisms and procedures.

3.2.1.2   Certification Practices Statement

A Certification Practices Statement (CPS) is a PKI-specific document. In a purely PKI environment, the RFC 3647-specified CPS may serve as the KMPS for a CA. In such cases, the CPS will follow the RFC 3647 format summarized in Appendix B.

3.2.1.3   Information Technology System Security Plans

All government organizations are required by OMB Circular A-130 to develop security plans for their major applications and general support systems. The use of the format offered in "Information Technology Systems Security Plans" (Section 4 below) will assist in the development of a security plan that incorporates key management information.[10]   Appendix D suggests key management inserts for a Security Plan Template.

---

[10] Note also that SP-800-37 also requires Information Technology Security Plans as part of C&A documentation.

3.2.2 Common KMPS Content

Regardless of the KMPS format employed, the document needs to include a minimum set of information. This subsection identifies the kinds of information that **should** be included in all KMPSs.

3.2.2.1 Association of KMPS with the KMP

The KMPS **should** identify the KMI to which it applies and the KMP that its content implements.

3.2.2.2 Identification of Responsible Entities and Contact Information

The KMPS **should** identify the organizational entities that perform the various functions identified in the Organizational Responsibilities section (Section 3.1.2.1.2). The individuals assigned to perform each key management role **should** be identified. Contact information **should** include the name, organization, business address, telephone number, and electronic mail address **should** be included.

3.2.2.3 Key Generation or Acquisition

The KMPS **should** prescribe key generation and acquisition functions. The functions described will normally include those identified for the *service agent*, or its equivalent, as described in the KMI discussion (Section 2.1.2). Key generation and/or acquisition **should** be accomplished in accordance with the guidelines contained in the key establishment section of this guideline (Part 1, Section 4.2.5). The scope of key acquisition includes out of band procedures for acquiring keying material (e.g., initial key encrypting keys for communication with key centers and service agents). The KMPS generally identifies:

- Any management organization, roles, and responsibilities associated with key generation and/or acquisition,

- Any standards and guidelines governing key generation/acquisition facilities and processes, and

- Any documents required for authorization, implementation, and accounting functions.

For organizations that employ public key cryptography, the KMPS **should** identify the certificate issuance elements of the CA (and its hardware, software, and human/organizational components as appropriate), as well as registration entities. Operating procedures and quality control procedures for key generation and/or acceptance of acquired keying material may appear either in the KMPS or in separate documents referenced by the KMPS. Documentation of the key generation process **should** also be included in order to establish a chain of evidence to support establishment of a trust root.

3.2.2.4 Key Agreement

Key agreement, as defined in Part 1, Section 2.2.2.5, involves participation by more than one entity in the creation of shared keying material. Public key techniques are normally employed to accomplish key agreement. KMPSs may prescribe the organizational authority and procedures for authorizing and implementing key agreement between or among partner organizations.

Within the context of a KMI, key agreement will commonly be implemented by *client nodes*, using agreement keys received from *key processing facilities*.

3.2.2.5   Cross Certification Agreements

Organizations having distinct public key certification hierarchies or meshes, but requiring secure communications between their domains may agree to cross certify the certificates issued by each organization. KMPSs may prescribe the organizational authority and procedures for authorizing and implementing the cross certification of keying material between or among partner organizations. Within the context of the KMI, any authorization for cross certification **should** come from the central oversight authority or its organizational equivalent. Cross certification will normally be implemented in the key processing facility or its equivalent.

3.2.2.6   Key Distribution and Revocation Structures

The KMPS **should** prescribe the organizational authority and procedures for the design and management of the organizational structure and information flow necessary to meet the organization's key distribution, agreement, and revocation requirements. The KMPS **should** include or reference guidelines for maintaining the continuity of operations and maintaining both the assurance and integrity of the revocation process. The KMPS **should** include guidelines for the emergency replacement of keys, compromise lists, and revocation lists as well as timely and the reliable routine dissemination of keying material. Both the initial establishment and subsequent changes to key distribution and revocation trees **should** be authorized by the central oversight authority and implemented by the key processing facility (or their equivalents) as described in the KMI discussion (Section 2.1.2). Additionally, prescription of audit and control of the distribution process is necessary in order to maintain confidence in the integrity of the trust root.

3.2.2.7   Establishment of Cryptoperiods

The KMPS **should** prescribe cryptoperiods for the keying material employed by an organization. Cryptoperiods **should** be approved by the central oversight authority, or its organizational equivalent, and **should** be implemented by the key processing facility and client nodes (or their equivalents), as described in the KMI discussion (Section 2.1.2). Guidelines for establishing cryptoperiods are provided in Section 8.2 of Part 1.

3.2.2.8   Tracking of and Accounting for Keying Material

The KMPS **should** prescribe the organizational authority and procedures for any distribution of, local creation of, and accounting for keying material required at each phase of the key management lifecycle (Part 1, Section 7). General accountability guidelines are provided in Part 1, Section 8.5. Responsibilities and procedures **should** be identified for central oversight authority, key processing facility, service agent, and client node entities of the KMI (or their equivalents). Any relevant accounting forms and database structures **should** be specified as required for:

- Keying material requests,

- Keying production authorization,

- The authorization of the distribution of specific material to specific organizational destinations for use in specific devices,

- Physical or electronic distribution of keys or related cryptographic materials,

- Receipts for keys or related cryptographic material,

- Reporting of the receipt of keys not accompanied by authorized transmittal information, and

- The destruction of keys or related cryptographic materials.

3.2.2.9 Protection of Keying Material

The KMPS **should** prescribe the responsibilities, facilities, and procedures for the protection of secret and private keys and related cryptographic materials. Requirements **should** be specified for central oversight authority, key processing facility, service agent, and client node entities of the KMI (or their equivalents). General guidelines for the protection of keying material at different lifecycle stages (provided in Part 1, Section 7) **should** be included or referenced in the KMPS.

Note that where keys and key exchange security mechanisms are integral to a FIPS 140-2 compliant cryptographic device or application, reference to FIPS 140-2 and any local physical security procedures may provide an adequate specification of protection practices.

3.2.2.10 Emergency and Routine Revocation of Keying Material

The KMPS **should** prescribe the roles, responsibilities, and procedures for the emergency and routine revocation of keying material. The KMPS **should** prescribe the roles, procedures, and protocols employed at the key processing facility for the generation of CRLs and CKLs for prematurely lost or destroyed certificates and keys or for compromised certificates and keys.

The KMPS **should** also specify the roles, procedures, and protocols employed by service agent and client node entities, or their organizational equivalents, for the timely and secure reporting of potential compromises. The KMPS should identify the key types for which revocation actions are necessary (e.g., not necessary for ephemeral keys). General guidelines for key revocation provided in Part 1, Section 7.3.5 **should** be included or referenced in the KMPS.

3.2.2.11 Auditing

The KMPS **should** prescribe the roles, responsibilities, facilities, and procedures for the routine auditing of keying material and related records. The KMPS **should** also describe audit reporting requirements and procedures. Auditing is normally a function of the central oversight authority or its organizational equivalent. Note that audit requirements will depend on the sensitivity of the information (including what is to be audited, the frequency of audits, and the frequency of reviews of different elements of the audit log). Note also that audits will generally be conducted in facilities containing servers, rather than facilities containing only client nodes. Conditions and procedures **should** also be included for unscheduled audits that are triggered by the observed and/or suspected unauthorized production, loss, or compromise of keys or related cryptographic material. General audit guidelines are provided in Part 1, Section 8.6.

Note that where keys and key establishment security mechanisms are integral to a FIPS 140-2 compliant cryptographic device or application, and the keys are relatively short-term and are employed for protection within a client node or between communicating pairs, it may not be practical or necessary to document or audit those keys.

3.2.2.12 Keying Material Destruction

The KMPS **should** prescribe the roles, responsibilities, facilities, and procedures for any routine destruction of revoked or expired keys required at all KMI elements. Zeroization conditions and procedures may also be included. Part 1, Sections 7.3.4 and 7.4 include general guidelines that **should** be included or referenced in the KMPS. Note that the destruction of keying material is not accomplished until all copies are destroyed (including backups and archives).

3.2.2.13 Key Backup and Recovery

OMB Guidance to Federal Agencies on Data Availability and Encryption, 26 November 2001, states that agencies **must** address information availability and assurance requirements through appropriate data recovery mechanisms such as cryptographic key recovery. The KMPS **should** prescribe, for each KMI element, any roles, responsibilities, facilities, and procedures necessary for all organizational elements to backup and recover critical data, with necessary integrity mechanisms intact, in the event of the loss of the operational copy of cryptographic keys under which the data is protected. Key backup and recovery is normally the responsibility of the central oversight authority, or its organizational equivalent, although mechanisms to support recovery are likely to be included in client node, service agent, and especially key processing facilities (or their organizational equivalents). Part 1, Sections 7.2.2.2 and 8.7.2 contain general key recovery guidelines that **should** be included in or referenced by the KMPS.

3.2.2.14 Compromise Recovery

The KMPS **should** prescribe, for all KMI elements, any roles, responsibilities, facilities, and procedures required for recovery from compromise of cryptographic keying material at any phase in its lifecycle. Compromise recovery includes 1) the timely and secure notification of users of compromised keys that the compromise has occurred and 2) the timely and secure replacement of the compromised keys. Emergency key revocation and the generation and processing of CRLs and/or CKLs are elements of compromise recovery, but compromise recovery also includes:

- The recognition and reporting of the compromise,

- The identification and/or distribution of replacement keying material,

- Recording the compromise and compromise recovery actions (may use existing audit mechanisms and procedures), and

- The destruction and/or de-registration of compromised keying material, as appropriate.

Part 1, Sections 7.3 and 8.4 of this guideline contain general guidelines regarding compromise recovery that **should** be included in or referenced by the KMPS.

3.2.2.15 Policy Violation Consequences

The KMPS **should** prescribe any roles, responsibilities, and procedures required for establishing and carrying out disciplinary consequences for the willful or negligent mishandling of keying material. The consequences **should** be commensurate with the potential harm that the policy violation can result in for the organization, its mission, and/or other affected organizations. While the procedures apply to all KMI elements, the responsibility for establishing and enforcing the procedures rests at the central oversight authority or its organizational equivalent. Consequences prescribed in a KMPS **shall** be enforced if they are to be effective. Note also that it is necessary to correlate compromise records and the associated audit logs to disciplinary actions that are taken as a result of violations of policies or procedures.

3.2.2.16 Documentation

The KMPS **should** prescribe any roles, responsibilities, and procedures required for the generation, approval, and maintenance of the KMPS. The generation, approval, and maintenance of KMPSs are normally the responsibilities of the central oversight authority or its organizational equivalent. The generation and maintenance of audit records are also normally responsibilities of the central oversight authority or its organizational equivalent. The generation and maintenance of registration, de-registration, revocation and compromise lists, and accounting documentation **should** be accomplished at the key processing facility(ies), service agent(s), and client nodes (or their organizational equivalents), as required by the KMPS.

4   Information Technology Systems Security Plans

Information Technology Systems Security Plans are required for general support systems and major applications by OMB Circular A-130. Key management information **should** be incorporated into the security plans for the Federal government's general support systems and major applications that employ cryptography.

NIST Special Publication 800-18 Revision 1 [SP800-18], Guide fo*r Developing Security Plans for Federal Information Systems* [SP800-18], suggests content for these system security plans. Organizations that have already developed security plans in accordance with [SP 800-18] can simply modify their plans to include key management. Key management-related additions to these plans are suggested below, and a template for an information system security plan is provided with key management enhancements in Appendix D.

4.1   General Support System

As defined in [SP800-18], general support systems are interconnected information resources that share a common direct management control and common functionality. General support systems normally include hardware, software, information, data applications, communications facilities, and people, and provide support for a variety of users and/or applications. Examples of general support systems include LANs, network backbones, data processing centers, tactical radio networks, and shared information processing service organizations. Most general support systems employ cryptography to support access control, authorization, information content integrity, and/or information confidentiality. Some systems employ cryptography for non-repudiation or similar assurance purposes. The improper generation or handling of the keying material associated with cryptography endangers or eliminates the security services that the cryptography is employed to provide.

4.2   Major Application Security Plans

As defined in [SP800-18], major applications are applications that require special management oversight because of the information they contain, process, or transmit; or because of their criticality to the organization's mission(s). These applications are systems that perform clearly defined functions for which there are readily identifiable security considerations and needs (e.g., an electronic funds transfer system). A major application may consist of many individual programs and hardware, software, and telecommunications components. These components can be a single software application, or combinations of hardware and software that are focused on supporting a specific mission-related function.

Many major applications employ cryptography to support access control, authorization, information content integrity, and/or information confidentiality. Some systems employ cryptography for non-repudiation or similar assurance purposes. As in the case of general support systems, the improper generation or handling of the keying material associated with cryptography endangers or eliminates the security services that the cryptography is employed to provide. Major applications can run on a general support system. In such cases, the major applications security plan **should** provide a reference in a Key Management Appendix to the appropriate general support system security plan. Otherwise, it is recommended that a Key Management Appendix be added to the plan. The content of a Key Management Appendix to the major applications security plan is identified in Section 4.3.

4.3 Key Management Additions to System Security Plans

According to [SP800-18], security plans for major applications and general support systems **should** include system identification information (including system purpose, environment, attributes, and the controls contained in NIST Special Publication 800-53 [SP800-53]). It is recommended that a Key Management Appendix be added to any security plan that identifies key management roles and responsibilities for systems that employ cryptography. Additionally, the following key management-related information and controls **should** be included in the bodies of the system security plans.

- *System Identification*: System identification information **should** identify configurable information security mechanisms. This **should** include the identification of security hardware and software upon which the security of sensitive information will depend. The functions of the mechanisms **should** be related to the information security services to be provided (confidentiality, integrity, and availability). Configurable information security mechanisms **should** also include the identification of configuration requirements for each security mechanism (e.g., key variables, firewall protocol and access settings, operating system and access control lists). The sources and managers responsible for configuration variables **should** be identified.

- *Control Families*: Cryptographic and key management material **should** be added for physical and environmental protection; configuration management; contingency planning, and system and information integrity control families:

  - Physical and Environmental Protection – This subsection **should** identify any cryptographic mechanisms employed, together with any applicable implementation or environmental standards (e.g., FIPS 140-2).

  - Configuration Management - This subsection **should** specify key management procedures. The subsection entry may simply refer to a Key Management Appendix).

  - Contingency Planning - This subsection **should** specify any key archiving and recovery procedures employed to support the recovery of encrypted files. This should include the location(s) of stored and archived cryptographic keys.

  - System and Information Integrity - This subsection **should** identify any digital signature or other cryptographic authentication or authorization mechanisms installed in the system. It **should** indicate whether or not digital signature and/or other integrity keying materials are validated (certification authority and completeness/correctness).

- *Access Control*: The subsection of the plan that addresses logical access controls **should** describe any cryptographic mechanisms employed, the applicable standards for their implementation and operation, and key variable sources and guidelines (may refer to a Key Management Appendix).

- *Key Management Appendix*: It is recommended that a Key Management Appendix be added to the plan that identifies key management roles and responsibilities. Some organizations may have well-defined key management infrastructures and up-to-date and comprehensive key management policies and practices documents. In such cases, the appendix may simply reference the appropriate sections of the documents that define key management policies, practices and infrastructure. In any event, the following information **should** be included in a Key Management Appendix, either in detail or by reference.

- Identification of the Keying Material Manager (The keying material manager **should** report directly to the organization's chief executive officer, chief operations executive, or chief information systems officer. The keying material manager is a key employee who **should** have the capabilities and trustworthiness that are commensurate with the responsibility for maintaining the authority and integrity of all formal electronic transactions, and the confidentiality of all information that is sufficiently sensitive to warrant cryptographic protection.)

- Identification of the title, role, or individual on behalf of which an organization's Certification Authority (CA) signs certificates (where applicable where public key cryptography is employed). This **should** normally be either the keying material manager or his/her immediate superior.

- Key Management Organization (Identification of the job titles, roles, and/or individuals responsible for the following functions:)

  ◆ Key generation or acquisition;

  ◆ Agreements with partner organizations regarding the cross-certification of keying material;

  ◆ Design and management of the key distribution and revocation structure,

  ◆ Establishment of cryptoperiods;

  ◆ Distribution of and accounting for keying material;

  ◆ Protection of secret and private keys and related materials;

  ◆ Emergency and routine revocation of keying material;

  ◆ Auditing of keying material and related records;

  ◆ Destruction of revoked or expired keys;

  ◆ Key recovery

- Key Management Structure (A description of the architecture for key certification, distribution and revocation within the organization. A description of the procedures for modifying the architecture and for establishing cryptoperiods.)

- Key Management Procedures

  ◆ Key Generation (A brief description of the procedures to be followed for key generation. This section includes references to applicable standards and guidelines. Some procedures may be represented by reference. Note that not

41

all organizations that employ cryptography will necessarily generate keying material.)

♦ Key Acquisition (An identification of the source(s) of keying material. A description of the ordering procedures and examples of any forms employed in ordering keying material.)

♦ Cross Certification Agreements (A description of the cross-certification procedures and examples of any forms that are employed in establishing and/or implementing cross-certification agreements.)

♦ Distribution of and Accounting for Keying Material (A description of the procedures and forms associated with requests for keying material, the acknowledgement and disposition of the requests, the receipting for keying material, creating and maintaining keying material inventories, reporting the destruction of keying material, and reporting the acquisition or loss of keying material under exceptional circumstances.)

♦ Emergency and Routine Revocation of Keying Material (A description of the rules and procedures for the revocation of keying material under both routine and exceptional circumstances (e.g., a notice of unauthorized access to operational keying material).)

♦ Protection of Secret and Private Keys and Related Materials (The methods and procedures employed to protect keying material under various circumstances (e.g., pre-operational, operational, revoked).)

♦ Destruction of Revoked or Expired Keys (The procedures and guidelines that identify the circumstances, responsibilities, and methods for the destruction of keying material.)

♦ Auditing of Keying Material and Related Records (A description of the circumstances, responsibilities, and methods for the auditing of keying material.)

♦ Key Recovery (A specification of the circumstances and process for authorizing key recovery and an identification of the guidelines and procedures for key recovery operations.)

♦ Compromise Recovery (The procedures for recovery from the unauthorized exposure of sensitive keying material.)

♦ Disciplinary Actions (A specification of the consequences for the willful or negligent mishandling of keying material.)

♦ Change Procedures (A specification of the procedures for effecting changes to the key management procedures.)

4.4 Documentation Required for Security Evaluation

Key management systems that support protection of Federal government information require certification and accreditation as specified in NIST Special Publication 800-37, *Federal Guidelines for Security Certification and Accreditation of Information Systems* [SP800-37]. Key generation, establishment, agreement, and transport mechanisms **shall** conform to FIPS 140-2. Data processing components of Information Technology (IT) systems employed in support of these key management functions will need to satisfy the operational environment requirements stated in terms of the *Common Criteria for Information Technology Security Evaluation* [ISO15408] where required by FIPS 140-2. Data processing components of IT systems that support other key management functions may also need to have been evaluated under the *Common Criteria*. (See NIST Special Publication 800-23, *Guidelines to Federal Organizations on Security Assurance and Acquisition/Use of Tested/Evaluated* Products.) The overall IT system or set of systems that perform key management for a Federal government organization is required to be certified and accredited under SP 800-37. The documentation required for certification and accreditation under SP 800-37, includes that specified under SP 800-18 Revision 1, plus a security assessment report and a plan of action and milestones. Where certification and accreditation of a key management system is required, the KMP and KMPS **should** specify conformance to SP 800-37 by validating compliance with key management control objectives contained in Appendix D of this document (i.e., SP 800-57, Part 2).

5 Key Management Planning for Cryptographic Components

Federal government organizations are required by statutory and administrative rules and guidelines to protect the confidentiality and integrity of sensitive information and processes. If cryptography is used to satisfy this requirement, it is necessary for developers, integrators, and managers to ensure that each cryptographic implementation satisfies all system security, compatibility, and interoperability requirements that are associated with the system into which it is being integrated. For any cryptographic device employed by the Federal government, there **should** be a specification of the keying material that the device requires, an identification of whether the keying material is internally or externally generated, a specification of keying material input/output interfaces, and a description of interfaces to any required validation process (see Part 1, Section 8 of this guideline). Development of the specification **should** be initiated before any cryptographic procurement is initiated. Algorithms, key lengths, cryptoperiods, key sources, and keying material access and handling requirements **should** also be specified (See Section 4). These specifications are required by system developers as well as by the managers of systems into which cryptographic components are integrated. They are also required by program managers who are responsible for the security of system implementations. Program managers who oversee the implementation of cryptography in Federal systems are responsible for ensuring that the systems include all necessary mechanisms, interfaces, policies, and procedures that are necessary to generate or otherwise acquire, distribute, replace or update, account for, and protect keying material that is required for system cryptographic operations in accordance with the guidelines presented in Part 1 and the policies and practices identified in Part 2 of this *Recommendation for Key Management*.

All cryptographic development activities and cryptographic applications programs **should** involve key management planning. In the case of planning for the acquisition and use of existing cryptographic devices or software, key management planning **should** begin during the initial discussion stages for cryptographic applications or implementation efforts. The planning **should** be evolutionary in nature, maturing as the cryptographic application matures, and **should** be consistent with NIST key management guidance. Key management plans **should** ensure that the key management products and services that are proposed for the cryptographic device or application are provided with adequate security, and are supportable and operationally suitable.

For cryptographic development efforts, a key specification and acquisition process **should** begin as soon as the algorithm and, if appropriate, the media and format have been identified. For the application of existing cryptographic products for which no key management plan exists, the process **should** begin as soon as the product is selected for the application. In both cases, the specification and acquisition process **should** be an initial step in the evolution of a Key Management Plan. For the application of existing cryptographic products for which a key management plan does exist, the existing plan **should** be reviewed in the context of the application's environment, and requirements and **should** be amended as necessary. Such a review process **should** begin as soon as the product is selected for the application.

The types of key management products and services that are produced for a specific cryptographic device and/or for suites of devices used by organizations **should** be standardized to the maximum possible extent, and new cryptographic application development efforts **should** comply with NIST key management recommendations. Accordingly, NIST criteria for the security, accuracy, and utility of key management products and services in electronic and physical forms **should** be met. The methods used in the design, evaluation, programming, generation, production, distribution, quality assurance, and inspection procedures for key management products and services **should** be structured to satisfy such criteria. The utility of key management products and services will be improved by employing uniform key management products and services, with a minimum of variation within each type of key technique, and by employing those types that have been accepted and successfully implemented by users.

Where the criteria for security, accuracy, and utility can be satisfied with any of the organization's existing suite of key management products and services, one of those products and services **should** be used. Where the application of current key management products and services results in reduced security, accuracy, utility, or added cost to a cryptographic application, then an organization may initiate efforts to develop and implement other key management products and services types, variations, and, as necessary, production processes. However, such efforts **should** conform as closely as possible to established key management recommendations.

5.1 Key Management Planning Documents

The document that describes the management of all key management products and services used by a cryptographic product (cryptographic engine, cryptographic device, cryptographic application, or user entity) throughout its lifetime is the Key Management Specification. Key Management Specifications are generally produced by developers or (where developers have failed to produce adequate specifications) by integrators. Organizational key management plans (e.g., Key Management Appendices to System Security Plans) document the capabilities that cryptographic applications require from the organization's Key Management Infrastructure (KMI). The purpose of these organizational key management plans is to ensure that any lifecycle key management services are supportable by and available from the KMI in a secure and timely manner. If a KMP exists for an organization, the Key Management Specification needs to be in conformance with the KMP. The KMPS **should** support both the KMPS and the Key Management Specification.

5.2 Key Management Planning Process

When developing a Key Management Specification for a cryptographic product, the unique key management products and services needed from the KMI to support the operation of the cryptographic product need to be defined. The checklist provided in Appendix E may be used to document information about cryptographic products used by an organization and, as applicable, their development and implementation processes.

Specification of cryptographic mechanisms, including key management mechanisms, **shall** necessarily take into account the organization's resource limitations and procedural environment. For example, an organization that lacks the physical protection facilities, security clearances for support personnel, and procedures and resources required for managing national security cryptographic material, might find it difficult to satisfy the policies and procedures required for the classified cryptography that is generally required for the protection of national security information. Before either approving or rejecting specifications requiring national security cryptography, the organization **should** consider the resource and operational implications of the decision. A contrasting example is that of an organization that must exchange information that is assigned a *moderate* or *high* FIPS 199 information security risk level specifying a FIPS 140-2 Level 1 cryptographic module. Such a decision could adversely affect the organization's ability to be permitted to continue to engage in mission-critical processing and communications partnerships.

The planning process must account for both availability of critical resources and for assurance requirements implied by the organization's critical mission functions.

5.3 Key Management Planning Information Requirements

The level of key management planning detail required for cryptographic applications can be tailored, depending upon the scope and complexity of the application. Obviously, if an organization's cryptographic support requirements are limited to e-mail security for a small number of employees, extensive planning documentation is neither feasible nor cost-effective. On the other hand, cryptographic security for a collection of networks that support thousands or tens of thousands of users require the kind of extensive documentation described in Section 4 and Appendix D. Regardless of the size and complexity of a cryptographic application, documentation of some basic key management characteristics and requirements is strongly recommended. Some basic information that needs to be documented for all applications is as follows.

5.3.1 Key Management Products and Services Requirements

The key management product and service requirements describe the types, quantities, cryptoperiod (lifetime), algorithms, and additional information that define the cryptographic application's keying material requirements. Cryptographic applications using public key certificates (i.e., X.509 certificates) **should** describe the class of certificates, and whether certificates and tokens already issued to subscribers will be used for the cryptographic application, or whether the cryptographic application will require additional certificates and tokens. If additional certificates and tokens are required, key management documentation **should** describe a rough order of magnitude for the quantity of certificates required. If certificates and tokens already issued (or planned to be issued) by the KMI are adequate for the cryptographic application described in the Key Management Specification, then the Key Management Specification **should** so state. Otherwise, any new or additional certificate or tokens features (e.g., new certificate extensions or formats) **should** be described.

The requirement information for the cryptographic application's key management products and services may be included in table format. The following information **should** be included[11]:

- The types of key management products and services (keys, certificates, tokens for various purposes),

- The quantity of key management products and services required (per device to be keyed),

- The projected quantity of devices to be employed in the application,

---

[11] Note that some of this material may be included by reference (e.g., distribution of cryptography by the using organization's KMI).

- The algorithm employed to provide each key management product and service being implemented (the applicable FIPS),

- The keying material format(s) (reference existing key specifications if applicable),

- Cryptoperiods to be enforced (a general recommendation or specific to application or organization),

- PKI certificate classes (as applicable),

- Tokens or software modules to be used (as applicable),

- Dates when keying material is needed (initial plans and plan revisions),

- The projected duration of the need (for applications or organizations)[12], and

- The anticipated Keying Material Manager (as applicable).

The description of the key management products and services format generally references an existing Key Specification. If the format of the keying material is not already specified elsewhere, then the format and medium **should** be specified.

5.3.2   Key Management Products and Services Ordering

A description of the procedures for ordering keying material within a specified KMI is required. Details **should** be included that are sufficient to permit a determination of the requirements for long-term support by the KMI.

5.3.3   Keying Material Distribution

Describe the distribution and transport encapsulation (where employed) of key management products and services within the cryptographic application. The distribution information will normally include when and where the key management products and services are encrypted or unencrypted, the physical form (electronic, PROM, disk, paper, etc.) and how they are identified during the distribution process.

5.3.4   Keying Material Storage

Documentation **should** address the method for storing and identifying keying material during its storage life (e.g., Distinguished Name). The storage capacity capabilities for key management products and services **should** be included.

5.3.5   Access Control

Documentation **should** address how access to the cryptographic application will be authorized, controlled, and validated for the request, generation, handling, distribution, storage, and/or use of key management products and services. The use of passwords, personal identification numbers (PINs), and their expiration dates **shall** be included. For PKI cryptographic applications, access privileges based on roles and the use of tokens **shall** be described.

---

[12] This can affect strength of mechanism, affect when the system must be replaced, etc.

5.3.6   Accounting

There needs to be a description of the accounting for key management products and services used by the cryptographic application. The use of logs to support the tracking of key management products and services generation, distribution, storage, use and/or destruction **should** be detailed. The use of appropriate access privileges to support the control of key management products and services used by the cryptographic application **should** also be described, in addition to the directory capabilities used to support PKI cryptographic applications, if applicable. There **should** be an identification of where human and automated tracking actions are performed and where two-person integrity is required, if applicable. Note that some of this material may, under some circumstances, be included by reference (e.g., reference to Department of Defense (DoD) Cryptographic Material System (CMS) documentation where the keying material is distributed by a DoD KMI).

5.3.7   Compromise Management and Recovery

How protected communications can be restored in the event of the compromise of keying material needs to be described. The recovery process description **should** include the methods for re-key or replacement. For PKI cryptographic applications, the implementation of Certificate Revocation Lists (CRLs) and Compromised Key Lists (CKLs) **should** be detailed. A description of how certificates will be reissued and renewed within the cryptographic application **should** also be included.

5.3.8   Key Recovery

Key recovery addresses how currently unavailable keying material can be recovered. A key recovery process description **should** include a discussion of the generation (e.g., whether or not the material was centrally-generated), storage, and access for long-term storage keys. The process of transitioning from the current to future long-term storage keys **should** also be included.

5.3.9   KMI Enhancements Requirements (optional)

The use of standard key management products and services provided by an organization's KMI is highly encouraged. Such use reduces the documentation requirements and facilitates both systems integration and logistics support. It also encourages the feedback of locally specific requirements to the KMI planning process. However, a cryptographic application may identify requirements that are currently not supported by the appropriate KMI. If applicable, it would be useful to address where improvements to the KMI are required in order to achieve the needed cryptographic application functionality. This will assist in identifying requirements for current and/or planned capability increments of the KMI. Even if a cryptographic application can be fully supported by the current or planned KMI, improvements to the KMI **should** also be identified if they improve the functionality of the cryptographic application, reduce user workload, or improve/reduce KMI functionality. Requirements identified can be analyzed for potential upgrades to the KMI, based on available cost, schedule, and performance constraints.

Appendix A: Notional Key Management Infrastructure (KMI)

This appendix identifies the elements of a representative key management infrastructure and suggests functions of and relationships among the organizational elements. This "notional" infrastructure builds on the Public Key Infrastructure (PKI), Kerberos, and US Government KMI components and mechanisms. The organizational elements and functions support all lifecycle stages of the keys necessary to the security functions identified in Part 1, Section 2.1, *Security Services*. Following the definition of KMI elements and functions, examples are provided for the distribution and management of both symmetrical and asymmetrical keys in a KMI environment.

A.1 Notional Key Management Infrastructure

This subsection presents a "notional" KMI as an example to illustrate common key management functions and requirements. A KMI is designed to incorporate a set of functional key management elements, or nodes, that collectively provide a unified and seamless infrastructure. Five distinct functional elements are identified for the generation, distribution, and management of cryptographic keys: the central oversight authority, key processing facility, service agents, client nodes, and user entities (encryption devices). Figure 2 illustrates a notional KMI structure.

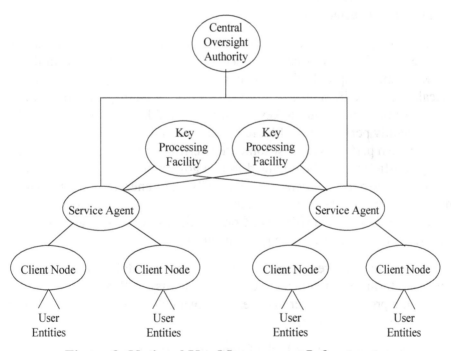

Figure 2: Notional Key Management Infrastructure

A.1.1 Central Oversight Authority (COAs)

The COA 1) coordinates protection policy and practices (procedures) documentation, 2) serves as the source for common and system level information required by service agents (SAs), and 3) may function as a holder of data provided by SAs. Examples of system-level data required by SAs may include: 1) product and registration information, 2) directory data, system policy specifications, and 3) system-wide key compromise and certificate revocation information. The COA is the central oversight authority that provides overall KMI data synchronization and system security oversight for an organization or set of organizations. As required by survivability or continuity of operations policies, the COA may be replicated at an appropriate remote site to function as a system back-up.

A.1.2 Key Processing Facilities (KPFs)

KPFs provide key production and storage services. These services include:

- The acquisition or generation of public key certificates (where applicable),

- The initial generation and distribution of keying material,

- The maintenance of a database that maps user entities to an organization's certificate/key structure,

- The maintenance and distribution of nodal key compromise lists (CKLs) and/or certificate revocation lists (CRLs), and

- The generation of audit requests and the processing audit responses as necessary for the prevention of undetected compromises.

An organization may employ the services of more than one KPF (e.g., for purposes of inter-organizational interoperation). KPFs can be added to meet new requirements or deleted when no longer needed. KPFs may support both public key and symmetric key establishment techniques. KPFs will typically serve as the source of symmetric keys for an organization. KPFs may also generate or obtain asymmetric or public key pairs. Where public key cryptography is employed, the KPF would generally perform most PKI registration authority, repository, and archive functions. The KPF also performs at least some PKI certification authority functions. Actual X.509 public key certificates may be obtained from a government source (government-managed certification authorities generating identification, attribute, or encryption certificates) or an external commercially managed certification authority (usually a commercial infrastructure/CA vendor that supplies/sells X.509 certificates). Commercial external certification authority certificates **should** be cross-certified by a government root CA.

KPFs may include intermediary redistribution facilities that maintain stores of products that are produced in physical form (e.g., magnetic media, smart cards). KPFs may also serve as a source for non-cryptographic products and services (e.g., software downloads for KMI-reliant users, usage documents, or policy authority).

All keys and products that originate at KPFs for electronic distribution **shall** be encrypted for the end user or for intermediary redistribution services before transmission. Keys that are manually distributed **shall** either be encrypted or receive physical protection and be subject to controlled distribution (e.g., registered mail) between the KPF and the user. Part 1, Section 2.3.1 provides general guidance for key distribution. A KPF may be composed of electronic and manual systems that generate a variety of cryptographic keying materials. KPFs **should** be designed to support legacy and existing system requirements and **should** be designed to support future network services as they become available. Some organizations may establish manual source KPF components that are capable of generating and producing human-readable key information and other key-related products that require physical distribution.

A.1.3 Service Agents (SAs)

SAs support organizations' KMIs as single points of access for other KMI nodes, including CNs and KPFs. All transactions initiated by user CNs are either processed by a SA directly or forwarded on to other nodes for processing. The SA directs service requests from its CNs to the KPF(s), and when services are required from multiple KPFs, coordinates services among the KPFs to which it is connected. SAs offer users a single interface point and common tools to order products and services, retrieve products and services, and manage cryptographic material and public key certificates. A SA may provide cryptographic material and/or certificates by utilizing product-specific KPFs for key and/or certificate generation. A SA that supports a major organizational unit or geographic region may either access an inter-organizational KPF or central KPF, or deploy its own KPF(s), as required, to support survivability, performance, or availability, requirements (e.g., a commercial external KPF that provides Certificate Authority services).

SAs may perform the following functions:

- Provide registration services,

- Provide directory services,

- Provide support for data recovery services (i.e. key recovery),

- Provide access to relevant documentation, such as policy statements and infrastructure devices,

- Process requests for products (e.g., user identification credentials),

- Assign and manage KMI user roles and privileges, and

- Provide interactive help desk services as required.

A.1.4 Client Nodes (CNs)

CNs provide interfaces for managers, devices, and applications to access KMI functions, including the requesting of certificates and other keying material. CNs interact with SAs to obtain cryptographic key services. CNs act as interfaces to end user entities (e.g., encryption devices) for the distribution of keying material, for the generation of requests for keying material, for the receipt and forwarding (as appropriate) of CRLs, for the receipt of audit requests, and for the delivery of audit responses. CNs typically initiate requests for keying material in order to synchronize new or existing user entities with the current key structure, and receive encrypted keying material for distribution to user entities (in which the content - the keying material - not accessible to the CN). A CN can be a workstation executing KMI security software or a FIPS 142-2 compliant special purpose device. Actual interactions between a CN and a SA depend on whether the CN is a device, a manager, or a functional security application. Examples of different types of CNs and their relationship to the SA follow:

- A *manager* CN might be a workstation operating KMI software that is used by individuals who have been assigned KMI management roles. Access to a SA through a client would generally require the user to be registered in (known to) the KMI and have one or more management assignments. A manager/user may choose to retain local records of KMI interactions, but the SA **should** retain records of all CN management interactions and may serve as the normal records repository for CNs.

- A *distribution management* CN would generally be capable of supporting product distribution from a SA and, where required by operational or organizational circumstances or key schemes, even provide local generation of some types of cryptographic keys. This type of CN can operate on a workstation or be integrated into a special purpose device. The distribution management CN would typically receive KMI products and services from a SA for distribution to a user equipment (i.e., the cryptographic device that uses the keying material). This type of CN might also receive and store products for future distribution.

- A *device* CN would usually be a KMI-enabled device (e.g., an encryption device or software application), known to the KMI (e.g., registered and in possession of a KMI credential, a certificate, or a transfer key), and capable of securely receiving keying material specifically for its use. These devices would be capable of interaction with a SA and might be capable of electronically receiving products directly from a SA. Typical interactions with a SA might include a request for 1) a key, re-key, and certificate revocation or 2) key compromise notification interactions. Distribution of keying material to a device CN might also be accomplished through a distribution management CN or a FIPS 140-2 compliant key transfer device.

- A *user application* CN would be a KMI-capable security application that functions on behalf of a user (e.g., a commercial e-mail application running on a PC that requires certification validation information from a directory service). Based on the roles and privileges of a user, the CN user application would access a SA and obtain required products and services. Interactions with the SA **should** normally be transparent to the human user. [In most cases, the user **should** be unambiguously and reliably identified to the application running on the workstation.] Interactions with the SA would occur automatically under the control of the cryptographically enabled application. Examples of user application to SA transactions might be an encapsulation type key recovery-enabled file encryption application's request for key recovery information, or an electronic mail application's request for directory information.

A.1.5   User Entities (UEs)

User entities are typically cryptographic devices that are employed on behalf of human users for encryption/decryption, authentication, digital signature, or authorization purposes.

A.2 Representative Encryption Key Lifecycles

Two examples of encryption key lifecycles are presented in this section in order to illustrate the possible functionality of interactions among KMI components. The first example is that of a key encrypting key in a symmetric key management scheme, and the second is a public key used in an asymmetric scheme. These examples are provided only for the purpose of illustrating KMI functionality, and not to illustrate key schemes themselves.

A.2.1 Example of Distribution of Symmetric Keys

In a representative symmetric encryption key life cycle, an agency may form a new operating unit within a division that will need to communicate with other operating units within the division and with operating units in other divisions of the organization. For purposes of this example, the representative or example key is a master key used for the generation of symmetric data encryption keys (DEKs). The user entity, an encryption device, is embedded in a FIPS 140-2 compliant smart card that is installed in a laptop computer with a desktop docking station.

The new operating unit is designated "Operating Unit #3 of Division A," (Ops A3). It will need encrypted communications with Operating Units #1 and #2 of Division A, and Operating Unit #1 of Division B (Ops A1, Ops A2, and Ops B1). Ops A3 will also require encrypted communications with the Division A management unit (Div A). All four *Division A* units are served by SA_1. *Division B* is served by SA_2. There is only one primary *Agency KPF*. The KPF has an arrangement with *Company XYZ* for *Company XYZ* to supply X.509 certificates that support RSA 2048 digital signature and key transport functions. *Company XYZ* issues certificates that incorporate the Agency identification only to the *Agency KPF*. *Company XYZ* will make changes to the certificate issuing policy only in response to requests from the manager of the *Agency COA*. The CNs are assumed to exercise distribution CN, device CN, and application CN functionality. Figure 3 illustrates the components in the symmetric key example.

1. At some time before the encryption key is needed by the operating unit, the *Agency KPF* generates a set of master keys that can be used by the cryptographic units in Agency-purchased smart cards to generate session keys. The representative key is one of these master keys.

2. The manager of the new operating unit, upon realizing that keying material is needed to support his organization's secure communications, requests cryptographic support by a hard copy request, endorsed by the *Division A* manager to be sent to the *Division A* Chief Information Systems Officer (CIO). The request includes the serial number of the laptop into which cryptographic material is to be installed.

3. The *Division A* CIO authorizes an SA_1 operator to send a request to the *Agency KPF* to issue CN software and a smart card (*Ops A3 user entity*) for use in the specified Ops A3 laptop, and that the smart card be loaded with the following cryptographic material:

   - A *master key* to be used by the *Ops A3 user entity's* key derivation process for the derivation of symmetric data encryption keys,

   - An RSA certificate that can be employed with the *Ops A3 user entity's* key transport process to decrypt data encryption keys received from other user entities (including SA_1),

   - The RSA private key associated with the key transport certificate,

53

- An RSA certificate that can be employed with the *Ops A3 user entity's* integrity process to enable other user entities to verify the signed key exchange and key management messages, and

- The RSA private signing key associated with the signature certificate.

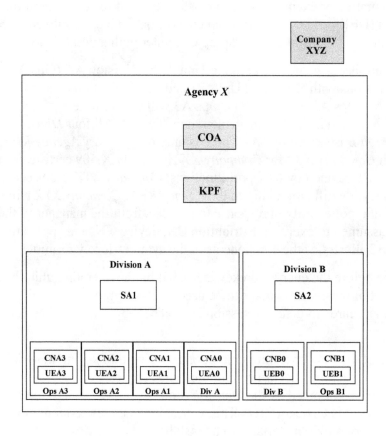

Figure 3: Distribution of Symmetric Keys

4. The SA_1 operator establishes a CN_{A3} audit record and enters the request into the SA_1 audit record. The *KPF* sends the software and loaded smart card to Ops A3. The *KPF* sends a record of the shipment to SA_1. The record of the shipment is entered into the CN_{A3} audit record at SA_1.

5. The Ops A3 user or his/her agent installs the smart card and *device client* software into the laptop previously identified to SA_1. When the material is installed, the Ops A3 laptop

becomes CN "A3" (*CN_{A3}*). *CN_{A3}*'s *device client* software automatically initiates a transport and digital signature certificate exchange with *SA_1* and issues a signed and encrypted receipt for the smart card and client node software.

6. *CN_{A3}*'s exchange of transport and signature certificates with the client nodes for user entities Ops A1, Ops A2, Ops B1, and Div A (*CN_{A1}*, *CN_{A2}*, *CN_{B1}*, and *CN_{A0}*); will enable DEK transport and signature verification that will support required encrypted communications with those organizations.

7. *CN_{A3}* will also use a DEK derived from the master key for file encryption purposes. Under this Agency's continuity of operations policy, this file encryption DEK **shall** be sent in encrypted form to *SA_1* for key recovery purposes, and back-up copies of encrypted files **shall** be stored separately from the laptop.

8. At some time in the future, the *CN_{A3}* laptop is lost or stolen. The user of the laptop **shall** immediately notify his division manager. The division manager **shall**, under the Agency's key management policy, notify the *COA* and *SA_1* that the cryptographic material contained in *CN_{A3}*/*user entity A3* is assumed to be compromised. Together with the notification, the manager requests (via *CN_{A0}*) that a replacement smart card, with necessary keys, certificates, and software be issued to Ops A3.

9. *SA_1* enters the identities of the compromised material into a CKL (for the master key) and a CRL (for the certificates). *SA_1* also enters the assumed compromise into the *CN_{A3}* audit log and archives CN_{A3}'s back-up file encryption DEK and certificates.

10. On receipt of approval from the *COA*, *SA_1* requests the replacement materials from the *KPF*, and steps 4 and 5 are repeated. *CN_{A3}* is now back in business except for the backed-up encrypted files.

11. *CN_{A3}* requests the archived file encryption DEK from *SA_1*.

12. *SA_1* decrypts the old file encryption DEK and re-encrypts it using the new *CN_{A3}* public key. *SA_1* sends the re-encrypted file encryption DEK to *CN_{A3}* and destroys the old DEK and certificates. The *SA_1* operator enters a record of the exchange and destruction into the *CN_{A3}* audit record.

A.2.2   Example of Distribution of Asymmetric Keys

In the asymmetric example, an organizational structure similar to that of the symmetric example is assumed. In this example, however, the Agency performs its own certification functions, independent of external sources (e.g., *XYZ Corporation*). The KPF generates certificates for keys generated by user entities within CNs. The KPF, SAs, and CNs have digital signature certificates. The CNs also have key transport public key certificates. Also in this asymmetric example, each CN includes two user entities (cryptographic devices). One of the devices performs key transport (among other encryption-related functions), and the other is used to generate and verify digital signatures. Figure 4 illustrates the KMI organizational elements involved in the example.

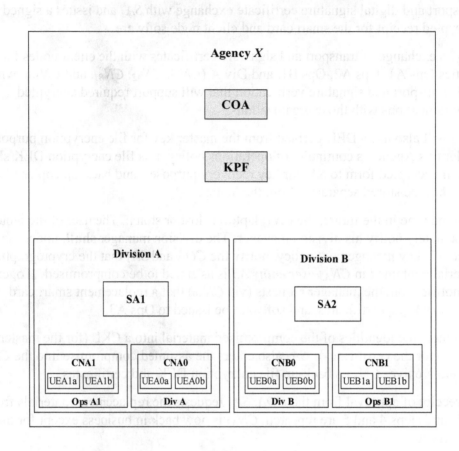

Figure 4: Distribution of Asymmetric Keys

1. The user of CN_{A1}, needing new keys to support key transport and digital signature capabilities, instructs his CN device software to have his cryptographic devices (UE_{A1a} and UE_{A1b}) generate public key/private key pairs. The key pair generated by UE_{A1a} will be used by that device for key transport operations. The key pair generated by UE_{A1b} will be used by that device for digital signature and verification operations.

2. CN_{A1} sends the UE_{A1} key transport public key and the UE_{A1b} signature verification public key to the SA_1 with a request for public key certificates. The request **shall** have integrity protection. Both CN_{A1} and SA_1 log the request in their respective audit records.

3. SA_1 forwards the request for certificates to the KPF. The forwarding message **shall** also have integrity protection assuring the KPF that the request was received correctly from SA_1. The forwarding of the request to the KPF is logged in the SA_1 audit records, and the request is logged in the KPF audit record as having come from CN_{A1} through SA_1.

56

4. The KPF verifies the request. Assuming that the request is verified as having been correctly received, having originated with CN_{A1}, and as having been forwarded by SA_1, the KPF generates certificates for the public key to be used for key transport and for the signature verification public key. The KPF signs both certificates using its signing private key and sends the certificates to CN_{A1} via SA_1. The issuing of the certificates is logged in the KPF audit record.

5. The user of CN_{A1} causes CN_{A1} to send the certificates to other entities with which the user of CN_{A1} will need to communicate securely (e.g., CN_{A0} and CN_{B1}). Note that the signing private key and the key transport private key never leave CN_{A1}. This preserves the potential for non-repudiation and secure key transport. Also note that users such as CN_{A0} and CN_{B1} will need to possess the KPF's signature verification key in order to establish the validity of the certificates.

6. After one year, the certificate for the CN_{A1} key transport public key expires. The KPF includes the identity of the key in a CRL and distributes the CRL. The KPF **shall** retain a record of the CRL and forward a copy of the CRL to the COA. CN_{A1} destroys the key transport private key, logs the destruction in its audit record, and sends a notification of the destruction to the KPF via SA_1. Records of the destruction report are logged at SA_1 and the KPF. It is assumed that a new key transport key pair will have been generated at CN_{A1}, and a request for a new certificate will have been forwarded to the KPF via SA_1.

A.3 Integration of the KMI Into Organizations

In the real world, organizations are not built around key management infrastructures; rather KMIs are integrated into existing organizational structures. Existing organizational relationships can affect the notional KMI. This can result in some duplication of KMI functionality within the organization and/or a division of the functions of notional KMI elements among multiple organizational elements. Figure 5 depicts a hypothetical organization. Note that the structure of the organization depicted is not a recommended structure. It is provided only to illustrate how an organization's underlying structure can affect the structure of a KMI.

A.3.1 Key Management Elements of the Hypothetical Organization

The hypothetical organization is assumed to have placed telecommunications responsibilities in its Information Technology Directorate rather than in an administrative or services directorate.[13] The Director of Information Technology is also the CIO. In this case, the CIO also serves as the organization's *COA*. General cryptographic support is obtained from the Information Services Division of the Information Technology Directorate. The *KPF* is located in the Information Services Division, and training for operation and maintenance of cryptographic components is also obtained from the Information Services Division. The hypothetical organization's

---

[13] This organizational idiosyncrasy is relatively common. In many technical organizations, in-house IT expertise and support facilities develop in the course of business or mission operations. Budget and other resource constraints then cause management to use these in-house resources for general organizational support. Often, IT support remains within the major administrative unit within which it evolved rather than being established as a separate dedicated IT capability within an administrative or facility support department. Budgetary and political considerations can dominate principles of administrative efficiency.

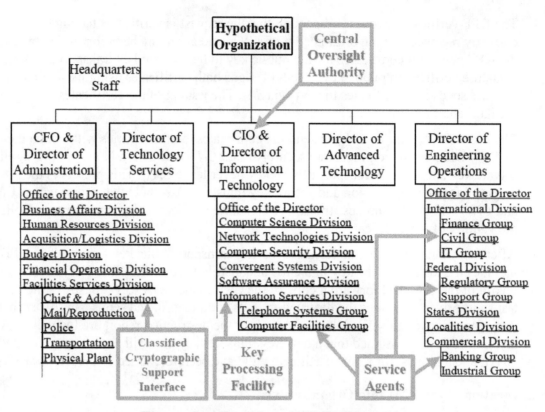

Figure 5: Allocation of KMI Elements

Information Services Division has not yet organized a cryptographic facilities group, so services and support are actually obtained from its Computer Facilities Group. *SAs* are supposed to be located at the *group* level throughout the hypothetical agency, though where organizations lack Service Agent hardware and software, they may apply to the Information Services Division for permission to use the Computer Facilities Group's capabilities.

Ideally, a single cryptographic services group would support all of an organization's key management needs. However, this is often not the case. In the hypothetical organization depicted in Figure 5, the element that originally processed classified Federal government information was the Mail and Reproduction Group within the Administration Directorate's Facilities Services Division. Other agency-wide personnel security, physical security, and police support resources were also assigned to this Facilities Services Division. So, even though other IT security management responsibilities fall under the Information Technology Directorate, the office responsible for requesting and managing classified cryptographic services is still that of the Chief, Facilities Service Division. Note that this activity is administratively independent from that of the KMI.

A.3.2 Key Management Operations Within the Hypothetical Organization

The hypothetical organization is assumed to use128-bit AES [FIPS-197] for encryption, 1024-bit DSA [FIPS 186-3] for digital signature, and 1024-bit RSA for key transport purposes. SHA-1 [FIPS 180-2] is the hash function employed with DSA. *CNs* generate their own symmetric keys for AES and distribute them encrypted under RSA. The DSA and RSA key pairs have three-year cryptoperiods. The hypothetical organization is assumed to possess a CA for certificate generation licensed from a vendor. The CA is operated by the Computer Facilities Group within the Information Technology Directorate's Information Services Division. The operators and facilities associated with the CA are also responsible for *CN* operator training, and for distribution and maintenance of *UE*s and other *CN* assets. Thus, these personnel and facilities are responsible to the Information Services Division Chief for carrying out *KPF* functions.

1. When a potential user is initially presented with a requirement for cryptographic services, the user (or an administrative functionary acting on the user's behalf) applies to an *SA* for the cryptographic application and related facilities and/or support.

2. On receipt of the request, the *SA* prepares and submits a request for service to the *KPF*. [Note that in the hypothetical organization steps 1 and 2 may be combined. For example, a *group* supervisor may decide that an employee should be using an application that includes cryptographic processes. The supervisor may direct an administrative assistant to arrange for the employee to be set up with the necessary capabilities. The administrative assistant may then, using a secure *client node* connection and *SA* software, submit a request for service to the *KPF* located in the Information Services Division's Computer Facilities Group.]

3. *KPF* personnel then take the following actions:

   (a) Obtain approval for the request from the *KPF* manager (Chief, Information Services Division. Allocate a *CN* for the user that includes the necessary cryptographic *UE*, associated software, and other software necessary to run the application for which cryptography is required. Copies of the request and approval action are provided to the COA (Office of the CIO).

   (b) Schedule training for the user.

4. At the time of user training, *KPF* personnel take the following additional actions:

   (a) Verify the identity of the user, requiring an authorization memorandum from the requesting group and two picture IDs.

   (b) Create a user account in the *KPF* server.

   (c) Assist the user in selecting a password/passphrase that will be used for encryption of private contents of a key profile diskette to be used in the user's *CN*.

   (d) Generate a DSA key pair.

   (e) Send the DSA public key to the CA. Encrypt the DSA private key and store it on the user's key profile diskette.

   (f) Use the CA to generate a certificate containing the user ID and DSA public verification key.

   (g) Add the DSA certificate to the user's account in the server.

(h) Cause the CA to generate an RSA key pair and RSA certificate. Retain a copy of the RSA certificate and private decryption key in the CA. Encrypt a copy of the RSA private decryption key.

(i) Add the RSA certificate and a copy of the encrypted RSA decryption key to the user's account in the server.

(j) Cause copies of the DSA and RSA certificates and the encrypted RSA decryption key to be sent to the CN and stored on the key profile diskette.

(k) Assist the user in adding additional information necessary to complete the cryptographic profile diskette.

5. Following training, the user is encouraged to change the password/passphrase prior to operational use of the *CN*.

6. Prior to entering into integrity-protected exchanges with other parties, the user causes his/her *CN* to send a copy of his/her DSA certificate to the other party(ies). This will permit the other party(ies) to verify that the certificate was generated for the sending party's ID by a CA with which the recipient(s) has/have a relationship and to verify the DSA signature of the data.

7. Prior to entering into encrypted exchanges with other parties, the user causes his/her *CN* to send a copy of his/her RSA certificate to the other party(ies) and requests that the other party(ies) send copies of their RSA certificates. This will permit each party to verify each other's RSA public (encryption) keys and to encrypt AES encryption keys.

8. In the case of encrypted exchanges the *UE* associated with each *CN* in a communicating pair generates an AES key, RSA-encrypts the key using the other party's RSA public key and sends the encrypted value to the other party. The encrypted values are decrypted, and the two original 128-bit values are exclusive-ORed. The resulting value becomes the AES key for the encrypted exchange.

9. After three years, the user's DSA and RSA certificates expire. The *KPF* includes the identity of the keys in a CRL and distributes the CRL. The *KPF* **should** retain a record of the CRL and forward a copy of the CRL to the COA. The user instructs his/her *CN* to destroy the DSA and RSA private keys, log the destruction in its audit record, and send a notification of the destruction to the *KPF* via the local *SA*. Records of the destruction report are logged at the *SA* and the *KPF*. The user will need to repeat the process described above (less the training component) prior to receiving replacement certificates and private keys.

Appendix B: Internet X.509 Public Key Infrastructure Certificate Policy and Certification Practices Framework

Where all keys employed in a system are PKI keys issued by a Certificate Authority that is part of the Federal Bridge, a PKI Certificate Policy (CP) may serve as the Key Management Policy (KMP), and a PKI Certification Practices Statement (CPS) may serve as a Key Management Practices Statement (KMPS). Where other types of keys are used, a separate document is required. The standard format for developing both the PKI CP and CPS is contained in RFC 3647, the Internet X.509 Public Key Infrastructure Certificate Policy and Certification Practices Framework [RFC3647][14]. The RFC 3647 format **should** be used for CPs and CPSs. As stated in Section 3.1.2, most of the elements of the RFC 3647 format are also applicable to non-PKI environments, though a number of adaptations are required to accommodate symmetric key management characteristics (e.g., identification of key management message and CKL profiles rather than certificate and CRL profiles called for by Section 4.7 of the RFC).

RFC 3647 proposes an outline with eight major sections and 185 second- and third-level topics.

The topics identified in this appendix are candidate topics for inclusion in either a certificate policy definition or a CPS. While many topics are identified, it is not necessary for a CP or a CPS to include a concrete statement for every such topic. Rather, a particular CP or CPS may state "no stipulation" for a component, subcomponent, or element on which the particular CP or CPS imposes no requirements. In this sense, the list of topics can be considered a checklist of topics for consideration by the CP or CPS author. It is recommended that each topic and subtopic be included in a CP or CPS, even if there is "no stipulation"; this will indicate to the reader that a conscious decision was made to include or exclude that topic. This protects against inadvertent omission of a topic, while facilitating comparison of different CPs or CPSs, e.g., when making policy-mapping decisions.

In a certificate policy definition, it is possible to leave certain topics, subtopics, and/or elements unspecified, and to stipulate that the required information will be indicated in a policy qualifier. Such certificate policy definitions can be considered as parameterized definitions. The set of provisions **should** reference or define the required policy qualifier types and **should** specify any applicable default values.

Although the same general format is used for both the CP and CPS, the two documents are very different in character and content. While the CP is a high-level document that describes a security policy for issuing certificates and maintaining certificate status information, the CPS is a highly detailed document that describes how a CA implements a specific CP. The CPS identifies the CP that it implements and specifies the mechanisms and procedures that are used to achieve the security policy. The CPS includes sufficient operational detail to demonstrate that the CP can be satisfied by this combination of mechanisms and procedures.

---

[14] The full text is available at http:// http://www.faqs.org/rfcs/rfc3647 html or from ftp://ftp.ietf.org/rfc/RFC3647.txt.

Each CPS applies to a single CA[15]. The CPS may be the overall operations manual for the CA. Specific portions of the CPS may be extracted to form the CA Operations Guide, RA Manual, PKI Users Guide, or other role-specific documentation. Auditors and accreditors may use the CPS to supplement the CP during reviews of CA operations. Note that a CPS does not need to be published. The combination of a CP and the results of an accreditation process are often sufficient for to satisfy the needs of most external parties. [PKI 01]

B.1 Introduction

The introduction provides an overview of the use of certificates to be issued under the CP and explains how to identify certificates issued under the policy (e.g., by an object identifier [OID] in a certificate policy extension or, in the case of a CA or a sub-tree of a hierarchical PKI that issues certificates under a single policy, the issuer name). The introduction also identifies the user community and major applications that the policy is to support, and describes the types of entities involved in the operation of the CA and the roles that they perform. Although not required by RFC 3647, the introduction may also include general security objectives (e.g., Items (b), (c), and (f) identified in Subsection 3.1.2.1.1). Operational entities may include CAs, Registration Authorities (RAs), subscribers and relying parties, overseers of operations, those responsible for maintenance of the policy documentation, and other key management administrators. Finally, the introduction contains contact information for organizations that administer the CA, maintain the policy documentation, and approve the corresponding detailed practice statements (i.e., CPS). This contact information **should** identify the telephone numbers or mail addresses associated with the organizations that perform these functions. The CP need not identify individuals.

B.2 General Provisions

The "General Provisions" section captures legal and general practices information, including the obligations imposed by the policy on the CA, its RAs, subscribers, relying parties, and repositories. This section describes the frequency of compliance audits, who performs the audits, the necessary qualifications for auditors, the relationship of the auditor(s) to the CA, topics covered by the audit, actions to be taken as a result of any deficiencies identified by the audit, and communication of the results of the audit. The "General Provisions" section also describes the obligations, liabilities, and financial responsibilities of the various PKI components and specifies legal jurisdiction and dispute resolution procedures. This section describes methods, circumstances, and destinations for the dissemination of the CP, CPS(s), certificates, certificate status, and other information. Finally, this section covers financial charges (e.g., fees, reimbursement, refund policies) and warranties (including limits on liability).

B.3 Identification and Authentication

The "Identification and Authentication" section describes the procedures used to authenticate a certificate applicant to a CA or RA prior to certificate issuance. It also describes how parties requesting re-key or revocation are authenticated. This component also addresses naming practices, including name ownership recognition and name dispute resolution.

---

[15] A large PKI may have several CAs that are practically clones. In such cases, it may be more efficient to develop a single CPS that applies to all the "clone" CAs. However, this specification must include separate information (e.g., location, contact information) for each CA within the PKI. [PKI 01]

B.4 Operational Requirements

The "Operational Requirements" section specifies requirements imposed upon issuing CA, subject CAs, RAs, or end entities with respect to various operational activities. This section addresses the following subtopics:

(1) Certificate Application;

(2) Certificate Issuance;

(3) Certificate Acceptance;

(4) Certificate Suspension and Revocation;

(5) Security Audit Procedures;

(6) Records Archival;

(7) Key Changeover;

(8) Compromise and Disaster Recovery; and

(9) CA Termination.

Within each subtopic, separate consideration may need to be given to issuing CA, repository, subject CAs, RAs, and end entities.

B.5 Minimum Baseline Security Controls

Minimum Special Publication 800-53 baseline controls are described in this section.

Procedural control requirements for recognizing trusted CA and RA roles **should** be described, together with the responsibilities for each role. The policy document **should** state, for each task identified for each role, the number of individuals that are required to perform the task. Identification and authentication requirements for each role may also be defined. Procedural controls **should** be designed to enforce the concepts of least privilege and separation of duties. No single individual **should** be able to generate a new CA key pair. Regular audit trail reviews **should** be conducted. Individuals who authorize the issuing certificates to a subject **should not** be relied upon to verify the subject's identity.

CA and RA personnel security controls **should** include 1) background checks and clearance procedures required for the personnel having access to security-relevant PKI facilities and processes, 2) training requirements and training procedures for each role; 3) frequency and sequence for job rotation among various roles; 4) sanctions against personnel for unauthorized actions, unauthorized use of authority, and unauthorized use of entity systems; 5) controls on contracting personnel; and 6) documentation to be supplied to personnel.

This section can also be used to define other technical security controls on repositories, subject CAs, RAs, and end entities.

This section **should** address the following considerations:

- Key Pair Generation and Installation (e.g., key sizes, private key protection, public key protection during distribution, quality control);

- Private Key Protection (e.g., FIPS 140-2 compliance, backup, archiving, entry techniques, activation/deactivation, destruction);

- Other Aspects of Key Pair Management (e.g., archiving, periods of use, tamper protection of archives);

- Other critical security parameters? (e.g., protection employed through life cycle);

- Computer Security Controls (e.g., Common Criteria rating/profile requirements);

- Life-Cycle Security Controls (e.g., system development and security management controls);

- Network Security Controls (e.g., use of firewalls); and

- Cryptographic Module Engineering Controls (e.g., module boundaries, FIPS 140-2 compliance).

B.7 Certificate and CRL Profiles

This section is used to specify the certificate format and, if CRLs are used, the CRL format. Assuming the use of the X.509 certificate and CRL formats, this includes information on profiles, versions, and the extensions used. The Certificate Profile component of this section addresses topics such as the following:

- Version number(s) supported;

- Certificate extensions populated and their criticality;

- Cryptographic algorithm object identifiers;

- Name forms used for the CA, RA, and end entity names;

- Name constraints used, and the name forms used in the name constraints;

- Applicable certificate policy Object Identifier(s);

- Usage of the policy constraints extension;

- Policy qualifiers syntax and semantics; and

- Processing semantics for the critical certificate policy extension.

The CRL Profile subsection addresses such topics as version numbers that are supported for CRLs and CRL and CRL entry extensions populated and their criticality.
[Note that the topics in this section may be addressed simply by reference to a separate profile definition, such as the PKIX Part I profile).]

B.8 Specification Administration

The "Specification Administration" section of the policy document prescribes who has change control for the document, describes publication and notification procedures for new versions, and lists the CPS approval procedures.

APPENDIX C: Evaluator Checklist

Evaluators **should** determine that key management systems conform to minimum baseline security controls contained in NIST SP 800-53. Additionally, the evaluators shall follow the assessment criteria contained in NIST Special Publication 800-53A [SP800-53A], *Guide for Assessing the Security Controls in Federal Information Systems*, and employ the evaluator's checklist for determining the adequacy of the policies and practices of key management systems.

C.1 Policy

The term *key management policy* has more than one meaning. Policy consists of the directives by senior management to create a key management program, establish its goals, and assign responsibilities. The term *policy* is also used to refer to the specific key management implementation rules for particular systems. Finally, *policy* may refer to matters such as the specific managerial decisions that establish key management infrastructures and the generation, distribution, securing, and accounting for keying materials.

C.1.1 Policy Content

Evaluators **should** ensure that the organization's key management policy documentation includes at least the following information.

- Statement of security objectives,

- Identification of the Keying Material Manager,

- Provisions for the assignment of responsibilities for:

  - Key generation or acquisition;

  - Agreements with partner organizations regarding the cross certification of keying material and/or key agreement, as appropriate;

  - Key distribution and revocation tree design and management;

  - Establishment of cryptoperiods;

  - Distribution of and accounting for keying material;

  - Protection of secret and private keys and related materials;

  - Emergency and routine revocation of keying material;

  - Auditing of keying material and related records;

  - Destruction of revoked or expired keys;

  - Key recovery;

  - Compromise recovery;

  - Disciplinary consequences for willful or negligent mishandling of keying material; and

- Generation, approval, and maintenance of key management practices statements.

The evaluators may also check to ensure that the policy documentation contains other information identified in the Sample KMP Format (Section 3.1.2.1.3).

C.1.2   Policy Characteristics

Evaluators **should** ensure that organizations have established the following three different types of policy: Program, Issue Specific, and System Specific. Some organizations may refer to these types by other names such as directives, procedures, or plans.

C.1.2.1   Program Policy

Evaluators **should** verify that the organization has established a *program policy* that performs the following functions.

C.1.2.1.1   Create and Define a Key Management Policy

Program policy **should** be clear as to the numbers, distribution, and sensitivities of various classes of keys required; and which resources – including facilities, hardware, and software, information and personnel – are required to implement, manage, and operate the key management program.

C.1.2.1.2   Set Organizational Strategic Directions

This may include defining the goals of the program. For instance, in an organization responsible for maintaining large mission-critical databases, re-keying, key update and key derivation strategies and key recovery issues might be specifically stressed.

C.1.2.1.3   Assign Responsibilities

Responsibilities **should** be assigned to the key management organization for direct program implementation, and other responsibilities **should** be assigned to related organizations (such as system administration and information systems security organizations).

C.1.2.1.4   Address Compliance Issues

Program policies **should** typically address two compliance issues: 1) meeting the requirements to establish a key management program and the responsibilities assigned therein to various organizational components, and 2) the use of specified penalties and disciplinary actions.

C.1.2.2   Issue-Specific Policy

Evaluators **should** verify that the organization's *issue-specific policies* exhibit the following properties.

C.1.2.2.1   Address Specific Areas

Topics of current relevance and concern to the organization **should** be addressed. For example, an organization's management may find it appropriate to issue a policy regarding how the cross certification of keys is to be authorized to permit secure communication with other organizations.

C.1.2.2.2 Be Updated With Sufficient Frequency

Policy modifications are likely to be required by 1) changes in technology, 2) changing perceptions if the sensitivity or criticality of an organization's information changes, 3) changes in security services that are required, 4) changes in an organization's information exchange structure, and 5) changes in national policies.

C.1.2.2.3 Contain an Issue Statement

The organization's key management roles and responsibilities, compliance criteria and determination methods, and points of contact for critical functions **should** be clear.

C.1.2.3. Systems-Specific Policies

Evaluators **should** verify that the organization's *systems-specific policies* exhibit the following characteristics.

C.1.2.3.1 Focus on Decisions

The decisions taken by management to enforce specific key management policies, such as defining the extent to which individuals will be held accountable for the protection of keying materials to which they have access, **should** be explicitly stated.

C.1.2.3.2 Be Made By a Management Official

The decisions that management makes, such as the cryptoperiod length or key archiving requirements, **should** be based on a technical analysis.

C.1.2.3.3 Vary From System to System

Variances in key management policies may be expected because different systems employed for information processing within and among organizations may process information having different levels of sensitivity, security service requirements, data structures, exchange requirements, and managers' acceptance of risk.

C.1.2.3.4 Be Expressed as Rules

Specify who (by job category, organization placement, or name) is permitted and/or required to do what (e.g., order, authorize, generate, or used keys, audit records, or other key-related material).

C.1.2.4 All Policies

Evaluators **should** verify that all of the organization's policies exhibit the following properties.

C.1.2.4.1 Be Supplemented

Because key management policy is to be written at a broad level, organizations **should** also develop or adopt practices, procedures, standards, and guidelines that offer users, managers, and others a clearer approach to implementing policy and meeting key management and information security goals. Practices, procedures, standards, and guidelines may be disseminated throughout the key management infrastructure via handbooks, regulations, or manuals.

C.1.2.4.2 Be Visible

The policy **should** be published in documents that receive adequate distribution. Visibility aids the implementation of policy by helping to ensure that the policy is fully communicated throughout the key management infrastructure.

C.1.2.4.3 Be Supported by Management

Without management support, the key management policy will not be enforced and the availability, flow, and security of the organization's information are likely to be severely impaired.

C.1.2.4.4 Be Consistent

Other organizational directives, laws, organizational culture, guidelines, procedures, and organizational mission need to be considered in the development and promulgation of an organization's key management policies.

C.2 Practices

Key management practice statements **should** specify how key management procedures and techniques are used to enforce key management policies and satisfy the organizations secure information processing requirements.

Evaluators **should** determine that key management practices documentation clearly and accurately specify the design and implementation characteristics of the organization's key management system and that the practices documentation is consistent with the key management policy documentation and exhibit the characteristics specified in C.1.2.2 for issue-specific and systems–specific policies. Evaluators **should** verify that key management practices documentation specify 1) the components, roles, and responsibilities associated with the key management infrastructure; and 2) the roles, responsibilities, and guidelines associated with essential key management functions.

C.2.1 Infrastructure Specification

Evaluators **should** determine that key management practices documentation defines any functional elements, or nodes employed by the organization for ordering, authorization, generation, distribution, protection, accounting, and use of the keying material necessary to support the organization's secure information processing requirements. The infrastructure **should** accommodate the functionality of the four distinct functional nodes identified for the generation, distribution, and management of cryptographic keys in Section 2.1 of this *Recommendation for Key Management's* "General Organization and Management Requirements." These four general node types are a Central Oversight Authority (COA), Key Processing Facilities (KPFs), Service Agents (SAs), and Client Nodes (CNs). It is noted that organizations may choose to combine the functionality of more than one node into a single component.

C.2.2 Essential Key Management Functions

Evaluators **should** determine that key management practices documentation specifies how key management procedures, and techniques are used to enforce key management policies and functional requirements. The practices documentation **should** be determined by the evaluators to clearly identify the organization's decisions with respect to cryptographic design and implementation standards, information sensitivity and criticality, and risk acceptance.

Evaluators **should** determine that the key management practices documentation describes in detail any organizational structure, responsible roles, physical facilities, and detailed procedures necessary to carrying out the functions described below.

C.2.2.1 Algorithm Selection and Key Size

Evaluators **should** determine that algorithms and key sizes employed to provide security services are FIPS compliant and conform to recommendations of Part 1 of this *Recommendation for Key Management.*

C.2.2.2 Key Generation or Acquisition

Evaluators **should** determine that key management practices documentation prescribes key generation and acquisition facilities, functions, and procedures. The documentation **should** identify 1) any management organization, roles, and responsibilities associated with key generation and/or acquisition, 2) any standards and guidelines governing key generation/acquisition facilities and processes, and 3) any documents required for authorization, implementation, and accounting functions. For organizations that employ public key cryptography, the practices document **should** identify the certificate issuance elements of the CA (and its hardware, software, and human/organizational components as appropriate). Operating procedures and quality control procedures for key generation and/or acceptance of acquired keying material may either appear in the practices document or in separate documents referenced by the practices document.

C.2.2.3 Key Agreement and Cross Certification Agreements

If the organization has key agreement requirements or requirements to *cross certify* certificates issued by each organization, evaluators **should** determine that key management practices documentation prescribes organizational authority, standards, and procedures for authorizing and implementing the cross certification of keying material and/or key agreement, as appropriate, between or among partner organizations.

C.2.2.4 Key Distribution and Revocation Trees

Evaluators **should** determine that key management practices documentation prescribes any organizational authority, facilities, and procedures necessary to meet the organization's key distribution and revocation requirements. The documentation **should** include or reference any guidelines for maintaining continuity of operations and maintaining both the assurance and integrity of the revocation process. Evaluators **should** determine that key management practices documentation includes necessary guidelines for the emergency distribution of keys, compromise lists, and revocation lists, as well as for timely and reliable routine dissemination of keying materials.

C.2.2.5 Establishment of Cryptoperiods

Evaluators **should** determine that key management practices documentation prescribes cryptoperiods for keying material employed by an organization. Optionally, the documentation may specify or reference procedures and criteria for cryptoperiod determination.

C.2.2.6 Distribution of and Accounting for Keying Material

Evaluators **should** determine that key management practices documentation prescribes any organizational authority and procedures required for the distribution of and accounting for keying material at each phase of the key management lifecycle. Evaluators **should** determine that key management practices documentation identifies all relevant accounting forms and database structures for 1) keying material requests, 2) keying production authorization, 3) authorization of distribution of specific material to specific organizational destinations for use in specific devices, 4) physical or electronic of keys or related cryptographic materials, 5) receipting for keys or related cryptographic material, 6) reporting of receipt of keys not accompanied by authorized transmittal information, and 7) destruction of keys or related cryptographic materials.

Note that not all keying material necessarily needs to be subject to special accounting procedures. For example, it may not be practical or necessary to maintain records for relatively short-lived keys (e.g., ephemeral keys), that are generated by user devices (e.g., user entities at CNs), and that are intended for use within the CN or are part of a communication between pairs users.

C.2.2.7 Protection of Keying Material

Evaluators **should** determine that key management practices documentation prescribes any responsibilities, facilities, and procedures necessary for the protection of secret and private keys and related cryptographic materials.

C.2.2.8 Emergency and Routine Revocation of Keying Material

Evaluators **should** determine that key management practices documentation prescribes any roles, responsibilities, and procedures required for emergency and routine revocation of keying material.

C.2.2.9 Auditing

Evaluators **should** determine that key management practices documentation prescribes any roles, responsibilities, facilities, and procedures required for the routine auditing of keying material and related records. Evaluators **should** include any conditions and procedures for unscheduled audits that might be triggered by the observed and/or suspected unauthorized production, loss, or compromise of keys or related cryptographic material.

C.2.2.10 Keying Material Destruction

Evaluators **should** determine, where applicable, that key management practices documentation prescribes, for all key management infrastructure elements, any roles, responsibilities, facilities, and procedures required for the routine destruction of revoked or expired keys. In some particularly sensitive applications, provisions may need to be verified for the emergency destruction of keys and related material to prevent 1) the exposure of sensitive information or 2) damage to or misuse of critical resources or processes.

C.2.2.11 Key Recovery

Evaluators **should** determine, where applicable, that key management practices documentation prescribes, for each key management infrastructure element, the roles, responsibilities, facilities, and procedures necessary for all organizational elements to recover critical data, with the necessary integrity mechanisms intact, in the event of the loss of the operational copy of cryptographic keys under which the data is protected.

C.2.2.12 Compromise Recovery

Evaluators **should** determine, where applicable, that the key management practices documentation prescribes, for all key management infrastructure elements, any roles, responsibilities, facilities, and procedures required for recovery from the of compromise of cryptographic keying material at any phase in the key's lifecycle. Compromise recovery includes 1) the timely and secure notification of users of compromised keys that the compromise has occurred and 2) the timely and secure replacement of the compromised keys. Emergency key revocation, and the generation and processing of notification lists are elements of compromise recovery, but evaluators **should** verify that the practices documentation also includes any procedures for 1) the recognition and reporting of the compromise, 2) the identification and/or distribution of replacement keying material, 3) recording the compromise and compromise recovery actions, and 4) the destruction and/or de-registration of compromised keying material as appropriate.

C.2.2.13 Policy Violation Consequences

Evaluators **should** determine that the key management practices documentation prescribes any roles, responsibilities, and procedures required for establishing and carrying out disciplinary consequences for the willful or negligent mishandling of keying material. The consequences **should** be commensurate with the potential harm that the policy violation can result in for the organization, its mission, and or other affected organizations.

C.2.2.14 Documentation

Evaluators **should** determine that the key management practices documentation includes the roles, responsibilities, and procedures for the generation, approval, and maintenance of key management documentation.

Appendix D: Key Management Inserts for Security Plan Templates

This appendix identifies a system security plan template and key management material that **should** be included in security plans. The template information has been extracted from NIST Special Publication 800-18 Revision 1, Guide fo*r Developing Security Plans for Federal Information Systems* [SP800-18].

Note that the following sample has been provided ONLY as one example. Agencies may be using other formats and choose to update those to reflect any existing omissions based on this guidance. This is not a mandatory format; it is recognized that numerous agencies and information security service providers may have developed and implemented various approaches for information system security plan development and presentation to suit their own needs for flexibility.

Though the information identified in the Key Management Appendix outline provided below (template item 16) may be distributed among other template elements rather than in a separate appendix, all of the information described in the Key Management Appendix **shall** be included in the security plan for systems that employ cryptography.

1. Information System Name/Title

- Unique identifier and name given to the system.

2. Information System Categorization

- Identify the appropriate FIPS 199 categorization.

3. Information System Owner

- Name, title, agency, address, email address, and phone number of person who owns the system.

4. Authorizing Official

- Name, title, agency, address, email address, and phone number of the senior management official designated as the authorizing official.

5. Other Designated Contacts

- List other key personnel, if applicable; include their title, address, email address, and phone number.

72

6. Assignment of Security Responsibility

- Name, title, address, email address, and phone number of person who is responsible for the security of the system.

7. Information System Operational Status

- Indicate the operational status of the system. If more than one status is selected, list which part of the system is covered under each status.

8. Information System Type

- Indicate if the system is a major application or a general support system.

9. General System Description/Purpose

- Describe the function or purpose of the system and the information processes.

10. System Environment

- Provide a general description of the technical system. Include the primary hardware, software, and communications equipment.

- Key management-specific information that needs to be included in this section includes identification of any cryptographic mechanisms employed (including key variable sources) and the location of stored and archived cryptographic key variables.

11. System Interconnections/Information Sharing

- List interconnected systems and system identifiers (if appropriate), provide the system, name, organization, system type (major application or general support system), indicate if there is an ISA/MOU/MOA on file, date of agreement to interconnect, FIPS 199 category, C&A status, and the name of the authorizing official.

12. Related Laws/Regulations/Policies

- List any laws or regulations that establish specific requirements for the confidentiality, integrity, or availability of the data in the system.

13. Minimum Security Controls

- Provide a thorough description of how the minimum controls in the applicable baseline are being implemented or planned to be implemented. The controls should be described by control family and indicate whether it is a system control, hybrid control, common control, scoping guidance is applied, or a compensating control is being used.

- Key management-specific information that needs to be included in this section includes: key archiving and recovery procedures in support of recovery of encrypted files; controls for validation of digital signature and other integrity keying materials (certification authority and controls for determining completeness/correctness); key management procedures for key generation, distribution, storage, and disposal; and applicable cryptographic standards and guidelines for all cryptographic mechanisms employed. This information may be included in a key management appendix.

14. Information System Security Plan Completion Date

- Enter the completion date of the plan.

15. Information System Security Plan Approval Date

- Enter the date the system security plan was approved and indicate if the approval documentation is attached or on file.

16. Key Management Appendix

1. ***Identification of the Keying Material Manager*** *(The keying material manager **should** report directly to the organization's chief executive officer, chief operations executive, or chief information systems officer. The keying material manager is a key employee who **should** have been determined to have the capabilities and trustworthiness commensurate with responsibility for maintaining the authority and integrity of all formal electronic transactions and the confidentiality of all information that is sufficiently sensitive to warrant cryptographic protection.)*

2. ***Identification of the management entity(ies) responsible for Certification Authority (CA) and Registration Authority (RA) functions and interactions.*** *(Where applicable: where public key cryptography is employed, either the keying material manager or his/her immediate superior **should** be designated as the organization's manager responsible for Certification Authority and Registration Authority functions.)*

3. ***Key Management Organization*** *(Identification of job titles, roles, and/or individuals responsible for the following functions:)*

   a. ***Key generation or acquisition;***

74

b. *Agreements with partner organizations regarding cross certification of keying material;*

c. *Key distribution and revocation structure design and management,*

d. *Establishment of cryptoperiods;*

e. *Distribution of and accounting for keying material;*

f. *Protection of secret and private keys and related materials;*

g. *Emergency and routine revocation of keying material;*

h. *Auditing of keying material and related records;*

i. *Destruction of revoked or expired keys;*

j. *Key recovery;*

k. *Compromise recovery;*

l. *Contingency planning;*

m. *Disciplinary consequences for the willful or negligent mishandling of keying material; and*

n. *Generation, approval, and maintenance of key management practices statements.*

4. **Key Management Structure** (*Description of key certification, distribution and revocation trees for encryption, signature, and other cryptographic processes implemented within the organization. Description of procedures for modifying the trees and for establishing cryptoperiods.*)

5. **Key Management Procedures**

a. **Key Generation** (*Brief description of the procedures to be followed for key generation. This section includes reference to applicable standards and guidelines. Some procedures <u>may</u> be presented by reference. Note that not all organizations that employ cryptography will necessarily generate keying material.*)

b. **Key Acquisition** (*Identification of source(s) of keying material. Description of ordering procedures and examples of any forms employed in ordering keying material.*)

c. **Cross Certification Agreements** (*Description of cross certification procedures and examples of any forms employed in establishing and/or implementing cross certification agreements.*)

d. **Distribution of and Accounting for Keying Material** (*Description of procedures and forms associated with requests for keying material, acknowledgement and disposition of the requests, receipting for keying material, creating and maintaining keying material inventories, reporting* *destruction of keying material, and reporting acquisition or loss of keying material under exceptional circumstances.)*

e. **Emergency and Routine Revocation of Keying Material** *(Description of rules and procedures for the revocation of keying material under both routine and exceptional circumstances, such as notice of unauthorized access to operational keying material.)*

f. **Protection of Secret and Private Keys and Related Materials** *(Methods and procedures employed to protect keying material under various circumstances, such as pre-operational, operational, revoked.)*

g. **Destruction of Revoked or Expired keys** *(Procedures and guidelines identifying circumstances, responsibilities, and methods for destruction of keying material.)*

h. **Auditing of Keying Material and Related Records** *(Description of circumstances, responsibilities, and methods for auditing of keying material.)*

i. **Key Recovery** *(Specification of circumstances and process for authorizing key recovery and identification of guidelines and procedures for key recovery operations.)*

j. **Compromise Recovery** *(Procedures from exposure of sensitive keying material to unauthorized entities.)*

k. **Disciplinary Actions** *(Specification of consequences for willful or negligent mishandling of keying material.)*

l. **Change Procedures** *(Specification of procedures for effecting changes to key procedures.)*

APPENDIX E: Key Management Specification Checklist for Cryptographic Product Development

The following key management-related information for cryptographic products development may be needed to determine and resolve potential impacts to the Key Management Infrastructure or other keying material acquisition processes in a time frame that meets user requirements. Yes/no responses **should** be provided to the following questions as well as additional information for each "yes" response.

1. Are unique key management products and services required by the cryptographic product for proper operation?

2. Are there any cryptographic capabilities to be supported by the KMI that are not fully programmable in the cryptographic product?

3. Does the cryptographic engine implement a software download capability for importing updated cryptographic functions?

4. Does the cryptographic engine use any non-key material KMI products or services (such as CKL/CRLs, seed key conversion, etc.)?

5. Does the cryptographic engine design preclude use of any FIPS approved cryptographic algorithm?

APPENDIX F: References

[EO CIP]   Executive Order, *Critical Infrastructure Protection in the Information Age*, 16 October 2001

[FIPS 199]   *Standards for Security Categorization of Federal Information and Information Systems*, Federal Information Processing Standard 199 (FIPS 199, National Institute of Standards and Technology, February 2004.

[FISMA]   *Federal Information Security Management Act (FISMA) of 2002*, Public Law 107-347, 17 December 2002.

[OMB130]   OMB Circular A-130, *Management of Federal Information Resources*, Appendix III, Management of Federal Information Resources, 8 February 1996.

[OMB6/99]   *Security of Federal Automated Information Resources*, Memorandum from the OMB Director, 23 June 1999.

[OMB 2/00]   *Incorporating and Funding Security in Information Systems Investments*, OMB Memorandum M-00-17, 28 February 2000.

[OMB11/01]   *OMB Guidance to Federal Agencies on Data Availability and Encryption*, 26 November 2001.

[PL106]   *Electronic Signatures in Global and National Commerce Act*, Public Law 106-229, 30 June 2000.

[PDD63]   Presidential Decision Directive 63, *Critical Infrastructure Protection*, May 1998.

[PKI 01]   Housley, R and Polk, T; *Planning for PKI*; Wiley Computer Publishing; New York; 2001.

[RFC3647]   Chokoni, S, Ford, W, Sabett, R, Merrill, C, and Wu, S; *Internet X.509 Public Key Infrastructure Certificate Policy and Certification Practices Framework*; Internet Engineering Task Force; Network Working Group; Request for Comments 3647; The Internet Society; November 2003.

[SP800-18]   Special Publication 800-18 Revision 1, *Guide for Developing Security Plans for Information Technology Systems*, National Institute of Standards and Technology, December 1998. [Draft revision posted August 2, 2005.]

[SP800-21]   Special Publication 800-21, *Guideline for Implementing Cryptography in the Federal Government*, National Institute of Standards and Technology, November 1999.

[SP800-23]   Special Publication 800-23, *Guideline to Federal Organizations on Security Assurance and Acquisition/Use of Tested/Evaluated Products*, National Institute of Standards and Technology, August 2000.

[SP800-37]   Special Publication 800-37, Federal *Guideline for the Certification And Accreditation of Information Technology Systems*, National Institute of Standards and Technology, Version 1.0, Initial Public Draft, October 2002.

[SP800-53]   Special Publication 800-53, *Recommended Security Controls for Federal Information Systems*, National Institute of Standards and Technology, February 2005.

[SP-800-53A]   Special Publication 800-53A, *Guide for Assessing the Security Controls in Federal Information Systems*, National Institute of Standards and Technology.

[SP800-60]   Special Publication 800-60, *Guide for Mapping Types of Information and Information Systems to Security Categories*, National Institute of Standards and Technology, June 2004.